ROAR
Strengthening business performance through
speed, predictability, flexibility, and leverage

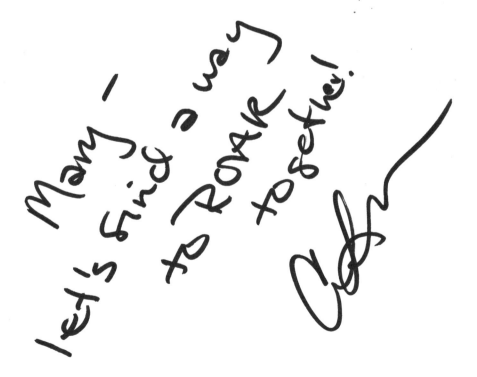

Mary —

let's find a way

to ROAR

together!

Also by Chris LaVictoire Mahai

THEM: The Handy Experience Manual

(with Linda Ireland)

ROAR

Strengthening business performance through
speed, predictability, flexibility, and leverage

Chris LaVictoire Mahai

Out of the Ordinary Media

Table of Contents

Acknowledgements   i

Introduction   iv

Chapter One

    Performance Chain   1

    Interview with John Dunlap, San Diego Zoo   19
    Director

Chapter Two

    Demand   30

    Introducing the 4 Lenses   47

Chapter Three

    Speed   50

    Interview with Steve Milligan, CEO, Hitachi Global   66
    Storage Technologies

Chapter Four

    Predictability   76

    Interview with Richard Davis, Chairman,   90
    President and CEO, U.S. Bank

Chapter Five

    Flexibility   98

    Interview with Beth Sparboe Schnell, President,   109
    Sparboe Farms

Chapter Six

    Leverage   118

    Interview with Leigh Abrams, Chairman and   132
    Former CEO, Drew Industries, Inc.

Chapter Seven

    The 4 Lens Profile   140

    Interview with Helen Ng, CEO, Planet Habitat   156

Chapter Eight

    Customer Experience   166

    Interview with Jim Notarnicola, Red Mango   174
    Executive, Investor and Entrepreneur

    Afterword   182

    Footnotes and Links   185

Acknowledgements

For a small book there are many people to thank.

I will start with Mike Verdin who is the originator (long before his Aveus tenure) of the early four lens concepts of speed, predictability, flexibility, and leverage that have been shaped over time and application. Mike, Layne Pearson and SS Yeow were the first contributors as I started this project.

Sue Gillman had the original idea for using animals to teach the concepts in this book through a simulation called *Taming the Performance Chain.*[1] In Chapter 1 you will be introduced to another idea that originated with Sue, the philosophy of 'See the whole. Mine the meaningful.'[2,3] It was the simulation and an article we wrote for Industry Week[4] that gave me the idea and courage to write this book.

There was a moment when I realized the huge need I had to make sure the animal facts and analogies in the book were true and accurate. I had a brainstorm and turned to one of my favorite organizations in the world: the San Diego Zoo. Several years ago I had the opportunity to travel with the Zoo. I reached out to a friend from that trip, Wendy Bulger, the General Counsel for the Zoo. Wendy not only took my call, she opened doors. From there I had the pleasure to work with Geneva Monge, my guide to all things Zoo-related (awesome and so attentive), Rick Schwartz, Animal Ambassador (wonderful, thoughtful and patient), Christina Simmons, Public Relations (kind and supportive), and John Dunlap, San Diego Zoo Director (brilliant and generous). I cannot thank the Zoo enough for their support of this project. Something I can offer: if you haven't visited the San Diego Zoo – go! If you ever have the chance to travel with them on one of their adventure tours, do it!

I need to sincerely thank each of the business leaders interviewed in the book. They were giving of their time and ideas, and *ROAR* would not be what it is without them. They are:

Chapter 1: John Dunlap, Director, San Diego Zoo
Chapter 3: Steve Milligan, CEO, Hitachi Global Storage Technologies
Chapter 4: Richard Davis, Chairman, President and CEO, U.S. Bank
Chapter 5: Beth Sparboe Schnell, President, Sparboe Farms
Chapter 6: Leigh Abrams, Chairman and former CEO, Drew Industries, Inc.
Chapter 7: Helen Ng, CEO, Planet Habitat
Chapter 8: Jim Notarnicola, Red Mango Executive, Investor and Entrepreneur

Then there is the photography.

The once-in-a-lifetime photograph you see on the cover and at the beginning of Chapter 2 is by Greg du Toit of South Africa. His must-read watering hole story is in Chapter 2 as well. I found Greg online. Through Skype and email I feel like I have made a friend. He is a gifted and generous human being. Give yourself a vacation and just dream through his website, buy one of his amazing photographs, or join him on safari. I keep looking at the calendar wondering when I can match up for one of his tours.

The cheetah and elephant photos were taken by my very dear friend, Dianne Ekberg Arnold. Dianne is a nature and travel photographer that combines her love of technology and nature into her art. Dianne also patiently went on a hunt for a perfect ant picture for me. We never captured one that we thought would work, so again thanks go to the San Diego Zoo for supplying the ant photo you see in Chapter 6.

The last great animal photo in the book is the coyote you see in Chapter 5 by Laurie Excell. Do you know how hard it is to find a great coyote photograph? Dianne referred me to Laurie and I'm so lucky she said yes. Laurie has to be one of the busiest photographers on the planet, but she took the time to help me and I'm ever grateful. See more of her incredible work at her website.[5]

Then there is all the work that goes into making the writer look good. For all their help I need to thank:

Katie Morrow and Karl Reichert for the cover design and all the graphics in the book.

Molly Danielson and Linda White for proofing and teaching me copy editing tricks. ("I think all these dashes should be commas; no that comma shouldn't be there; now I think that really should be a dash!")

Linda Ireland for all her wisdom and guidance and endless support through this process and launch of this book, as well as her incredible picture leading into Chapter 8, Customer Experience.[6]

Joanne McGowan for being the most persistent and challenging reader. Her questions and unwillingness to let me off the hook made a huge difference.

And, Daniel Mahai who has lived with all my big ideas and projects for years. He is the first person I turn to for a true read and clear opinion. He would tell you I ask his perspective just to do the opposite but that really isn't true. And, since I know he would rather I say less than more, I'll stop here, for him.

Introduction

ROAR is intended to get you thinking. Any good book does that, I know, but I mean it is intended to help you think about your business, your performance chain, your opportunities for improvement, and the experiences you deliver to your customers in new ways. It is not meant to fill you full of my answers for your organization, but instead to help you find your own answers. You will see more questions than answers in here – on purpose.

ROAR is a philosophy book of sorts, not a how-to book. Sure there are suggestions for finding answers to challenges that you face, but the book is not formulaic in the way some business tomes are. It lays out four 'lenses,' as we call them at Aveus,[7] that we know to be true guides for driving better outcomes through any performance chain. The four lenses are speed, predictability, flexibility, and leverage.

There are no case studies and no benchmarking statistics because this book is about what you are doing in your business, not what others are doing in theirs. There are, however, seven fascinating interviews throughout the book that add other perspectives about how speed, predictability, flexibility, and leverage show up in performance chains. These discussions allow you to see how other leaders think about, make decisions about, and adapt their businesses based on the concepts shared in *ROAR*. I am deeply grateful to John Dunlap of the San Diego Zoo, Steve Milligan of Hitachi Global Storage Technologies, Richard Davis of U.S. Bank, Beth Sparboe Schnell of Sparboe Farms, Leigh Abrams of Drew Industries, Helen Ng of Planet Habitat, and Jim Notarnicola of Red Mango for their contributions to this book.

In the case of demand (Chapter 2), an amazing true story is imbedded in the chapter just as we all need to be immersed in understanding demand for our products and services. Read about Greg du Toit's adventure and you'll see what I mean.

Finally, several years ago a colleague, Sue Gillman, came up with an idea for a simulation that would demonstrate performance chain problems and solutions in minutes. We created *Taming the Performance Chain* using animals to introduce the four lenses discussed in this book.

Since it is often difficult to get stakeholders together in one room to participate in a simulation, I had the idea for this book. Besides, it gave me a great excuse to combine three loves of mine: animals, adventure and solving business challenges.

I hope you enjoy the read and that you find helpful ideas in here. Even more, I wish you *ROAR*ing success in your own business adventures!

Chapter 1
Performance Chain

A cheetah, a coyote, an elephant, and an ant are called into a CEO's office. Sounds like the beginning of a bad joke, doesn't it?

The CEO has called an operations review meeting. She's upset. The company is falling behind. Not making its numbers. Analysts are critical of market performance. Customer satisfaction is down. Even though there are pockets of good work, the whole company is not where it should be. Overall performance is down. This is no joke. Some version of this discussion is happening in most companies around the world. The basic reality: we should be doing better.

Rashida Cheetah says, "Geez boss, I'm running as fast as I can – we have the fastest cats out there - we can't amp up our **speed** any more. The problem is these other guys."

Oralee Elephant says, "I KNEW you were going to blame it on us. Sure – just keep going faster and faster and expect us to keep everything on the rails, production problems down. Well, I know from my long memory that our product and service **predictability** has never been better."

Ace Coyote, listening to the cheetah and elephant argue, chimes in, "You're both idiots. The problem isn't going faster or consistent output; the problem is that the market has changed. Customers want something different – just delivering what we have been producing faster and more accurately doesn't matter if nobody is buying. I've got the most **flexible** guys in the world doing cartwheels to adapt your output into something we can actually sell!"

At this point, **Rickie Ant** just says, "Boss, I'm tired. We keep having these same arguments and our answer is always to pile on more. Well, even though I'm small, I carry my load and then some. I've recruited millions of my cousins to help. We have **leveraged** every asset we have to the hilt. We don't waste a thing, and we are holding this place together. But at some point, this whole hill is going to collapse."

In this storyline and throughout this book the cheetah represents speed, the elephant predictability, the coyote flexibility, and the ant leverage. You'll learn why these chosen characters are more than simple icons. But for now, let's leave them arguing with each other. We will meet up with them later.

Instead, think about meetings in your own organization with functional leaders trying to solve a performance challenge. The conversation may be with the heads of supply, manufacturing, service delivery, finance, and marketing. One is more worried about speed and throughput. Another wants to focus on quality and reliability. Customer and market requirements are on the agenda of yet another. And others raise concerns about the company infrastructure and the need to do more with less. Each one may be telling the story – accurately – from their seat and perspective and yet, the stories do not add up.

Q: What is missing?
A: A clear view of the customer problem to be solved and the performance chain to do it.

What do I mean by that?

Problem versus product or service: Too often companies start with the product or service they sell and get out of step with the customer problem they are solving. Opportunities start with a customer need. The need might be hunger, getting from city A to city B, learning a new language, work collaboration, financing a new purchase, or a million other possibilities. Any of those needs can be solved with a variety of products or services. When we start the performance chain with the product, we miss that first opportunity to think broadly about the customer and how to connect with them beyond the specific thing we do: fly a plane, rent cars, produce food, build and install technology, or offer loans.

That first misstep or narrow focus allows for both over-building and under-building of capabilities that ultimately will detract from performance. More about that later.

Performance chain versus functional responsibilities: If you ask most people to describe their organization, they will describe the org chart, the key functions, the top down or networked chain of command. Some may even describe the flow or linkages from one area of responsibility to another.

When you're talking to any functional leader, they will typically start with what they know – their area of expertise – and then wrap the rest of the organization and hierarchy around them to explain the company and what they do. This is human nature. Start with what you know and build out from there. Kind of like those maps you see in Time Square souvenir shops that depict the United States from the view of New York City. New York takes up about 85% of the picture and the rest of the cities, counties, states, 300+ million people and thousands of businesses, miles of farm land and animals, domestic and wild, trees, rivers, lakes, and mountains are all squished into the rest of the view.

It is one view – funny, maybe even poignant – but not really very helpful.

In a manufacturing or product sales organization a functional view may be something like:

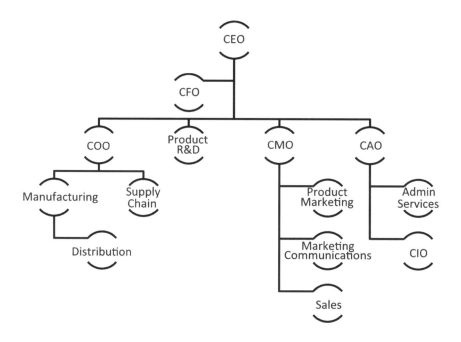

In a services organization a functional view may be something like:

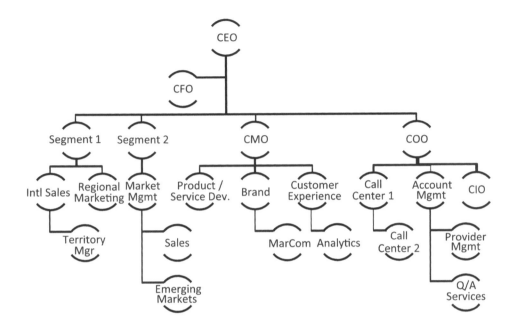

Some companies do all these functions in-house. Some focus on their "core capabilities" and outsource the rest. Either can be perfectly fine, and we'll look at both as we learn to tame the performance chain.

To build more effective organizations, we need a better way to see the work we do. We need a clear and accurate unbiased view across the company. Flow-based versus functionally-based. We need to understand the intersections of work, not the baton pass from one area to another.

That is what this book is all about: driving the best possible outcomes for your customers and your business. We will explore how you can use the lenses of speed, predictability, flexibility, and leverage to control your performance chain rather than it controlling you.

Throughout this book we will focus on understanding what drives peak performance against the customer problem you've chosen to solve.

Q: So – what is a performance chain?

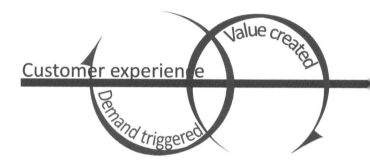

A: We define a performance chain as all the tangible and intangible elements that have to move from the moment you trigger demand until you have cash in the bank; all the ins and outs that have to work together and align to your target customer experience to drive the outcomes you want.

When you boil it down to simple terms, a performance chain is really just a system of moving pieces. It's about flow. Everything has an in and an out. Companies can be viewed across the flow of work and critical zones of work can be viewed based on an integrated understanding of the work – including all the functions involved.

In a picture, what does a 'whole' performance chain look like?

A performance chain can take a variety of shapes, but in its highest and simplest form it is a look across the organization as value is being created. Remember: from the time demand is triggered until there is cash in the bank. The basic zones may be something like this:

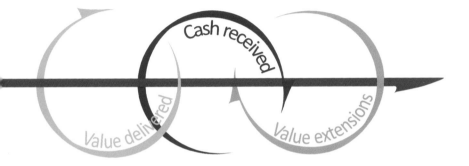

Highly complex or diversified organizations may have multiple levels of performance chains. Any value-creating process can be mapped this way whether a company has one or ten or hundreds of performance chains. Each has a sequence that can be mapped and evaluated for speed, predictability, flexibility, and leverage. Focus too much on individual elements or functions prematurely and you get hung up in the details. As a result, you'll be less efficient and may even miss the mark completely. You may create a high-performing cell or unit but the entire company – and most importantly the customer – may not benefit at all. When you concentrate on the entire system, the flow of tangible and intangible elements moving in and out, it gives you have a much better chance of peak performance.

If there are improvements to be made – and there almost always are – taking a full performance chain view allows you to have the greatest impact with your limited resources. Think of it this way:

See the whole. Mine the meaningful.

Through our individual educations we are conditioned to be problem-solvers. Business amplifies this orientation through localized accountabilities. So our instinct is to act. We see a glitch or a problem, and we rush to correct it. That desire to solve is admirable, and even helpful, but often masks the real source of the issue and very often will create another – maybe more troublesome – glitch down the line.

In the most challenging cases, you create dueling solutions or waste valuable resources as each functional area points to others as the source of the problem. Recall from page one the cheetah's singular focus on speed in conflict with the elephant, coyote and ant's perspectives.

Think about the organizational squabbles you may have faced, for example, between those responsible for driving demand (typically sales and marketing) and those responsible for producing and distributing solutions while holding down costs (typically supply and manufacturing or service delivery).

'See the whole' means exactly that: when you want to drive peak performance – top line revenue and bottom line profit – resist the temptation to act before you've got a clear, full view and options for improvement. Once you have that, mine the most meaningful actions to get performance on a better path. Most of these actions can and should be decentralized or localized so those closest to the work are directly involved and learn their contributions to the overall flow and creation of customer value.

This work doesn't have to take years or even months of analysis by armies of consultants and analysts. We will explore making improvements to the performance chain through the four lenses of speed, predictability, flexibility, and leverage later. Before that, however, you need to sign up for the benefits of having a clear overarching view of value creation across your organization.

The performance chain definition talks about tangible and intangible elements. Here are a few examples of each:

Tangible examples:

- People: staff, contractors, business partners, vendors, suppliers – all those individuals who contribute to the flow of work in your organization. Each person, regardless of position, can characterize their ins and outs.
- Parts or inventory: raw, partial and finished goods
- Service components
- Equipment: maybe machines in a factory; trucks, trains, planes and boats for logistics; work stations in a call center; bins and floor robots in a warehouse
- Tools: cash registers, phones, white boards, boxes, packaging
- Technologies: floor systems, planning, accounting, communications
- Geography and physical locations

Intangible examples:

- Data or transactions
- Policies, procedures, or work rules
- Decisions
- Actions
- Methods (often historical & maybe unwritten – "we've always done it this way here")
- Knowledge or expertise
- Communications

Every organization has a performance chain. When you think about your company, what do you see? Maybe a manufacturing plant or a series of them. A hospital or clinic. A network of distribution hubs. Call centers. Maybe a collection of branch offices or stores. People working in offices or from home or remote locations. We tend to most easily see the tangible aspects of our business. These are the anchors of your performance chain, your physical assets. They can and do change over time – and that is a very good thing.

The intangible aspects of performance chains are equally important, but often harder to imagine and can easily be overlooked. Policies, work rules, communications and hierarchy, to name just a few, drive the ins and outs. Without them, people sit idle. Machines rust. Production stops.

If you are a CEO, COO, a division leader, or a functional leader, can you visualize your company's performance chain from beginning to end? The flow of work as it moves through your organization? Not just the part you manage – the whole thing. Not by function or department or unit – but the way your company builds value as work moves through your system. The way people move in and out. The way ideas move in and out – or die before implementation.

What actions cause your inputs and outputs to flow? What actions get in the way, cause flow to bog down or stop completely? These actions may be human – or behavioral. They very likely are also designed into your equipment and the way your physical system works.

Do you know where your performance chain is truly strong and where it needs some improvement? Are you confident that all your investments contribute to solving your customers' needs – without waste?

What we are really doing in a performance chain view is tracking the flow of the answer to a customer problem as it moves across your organization. How does whatever the customer wants to buy from you move through your operations? How well does it meet requirements when received?

There are lots of questions to unpack. The 4 Lens Profile we introduce in this book (speed, predictability, flexibility, and leverage) will help you do exactly that.

If, as you are reading, you don't know or aren't sure of the answers to the questions above for your organization, you are not alone. Keep reading for some new ways to think about your possible answers. If you think you know and like your answers, keep reading and see if these four lenses don't help you with deeper insights. Before we get there, let's take a little field trip to bring the concept of a performance chain to life.

In some organizations performance chains are a real zoo. Literally. So, let's visit one of the most famous and successful in the world: the San Diego Zoo. Our trip takes us to the heart of San Diego where the Zoo sits surrounded by beautiful Balboa Park.

The Zoo is a cornerstone in the larger San Diego Zoo Global organization. Here is the way San Diego Zoo Global, the parent organization, describes itself on its website:

San Diego Zoo Global is a not-for-profit organization that operates the San Diego Zoo, the San Diego Zoo Safari Park, and San Diego Zoo Institute for Conservation Research. The Zoo was founded on October 2, 1916, by Harry M. Wegeforth, M.D.

San Diego Zoo Global is the largest Zoological membership association in the world, with more than 250,000 member households and 130,000 child memberships, representing more than a half million people. Both Zoo and Park are open every day of the year.

Mission Statement: San Diego Zoo Global is a conservation, education, and recreation organization dedicated to the reproduction, protection, and exhibition of animals, plants, and their habitats.

"It Began with a Roar" by H.M. Wegeforth and N. Morgan[8]

As the Zoo prepares for its 100th birthday, it is worth looking back at its start and understanding its incredible, successful journey to today. It is the rare organization that combines vision and will to both innovate and act as a steward of precious resources over the arch of a century. It is one of the reasons I wanted to start this book here. It is not just that the Zoo is successful today. It has been successful for 100 years.

It's worth a side trip to learn more.

To get you started: "We like to say the Zoo "began with a roar" in 1916 when our founder, Dr. Harry Wegeforth, heard the roar of caged lions that were part of the 1915-16 Panama-California Exposition in Balboa Park. Dr. Harry, as he was affectionately called, decided then and there that San Diego was ready for a zoo and later convinced the city to follow his lead.[9]

San Diego Zoo – as it is described today

The 100-acre (40-hectare) Zoo is home to over 4,000 rare and endangered animals representing more than 800 species and subspecies, and a prominent botanical collection with more than 700,000 exotic plants. It is located just north of downtown San Diego in Balboa Park.

Suffice it to say the Zoo has a lot going on and virtually no downtime – ever. Based on their description, the list of complicating factors could be endless, but let's just list some of the most obvious ins and outs that create performance challenges that San Diego Zoo faces every single day:

People – just to name a few:

> 500,000+ members
> Millions of visitors of all ages who show up 365 days a year
> Curators and animal keepers who work directly with the animals
> Guest services who work directly with visitors and members
> Researchers and scientists working locally and globally on issues of conservation

The most precious of tangible resources:

> Over 4,000 rare and endangered animals representing more than 800 species, each requiring individual care and attention
> 700,000+ rare and exotic plants in the botanical collection throughout the Zoo

The 100-acre Zoo with its own operating and support requirements

Food, medicine, water, power – for animals and people

Transportation in and around each facility and globally to natural habitats and other partner organizations

Facilities – the buildings, enclosures, pathways, public restrooms, shops, cameras and security, visitor information, websites, education, etc...

This is an organization built upon integrating new ideas every day since October 2, 1916. New ways of:

Feeding and caring for animals

Designing habitats

Managing transportation

Viewing for visitors and study for researchers and keepers

Researching locally and abroad, alone and with partners

Recycling and sustainability

Intangibles show up in the Zoo's innovative methods behind everything it does. They can be found in the:

Atmosphere – the hum of energy and life everywhere you go

Music – you may not even be aware of it but it is impacting your experience

Quiet – encouraged as dozens of onlookers converge to watch a mother and newborn

Guide's enthusiasm – sharing a story they've told a thousand times – knowing you are hearing it for the first time

Now, like any business, you can look at the San Diego Zoo functionally – animal curators, food service, transportation, technology, retail, security, etc. You also can study each facility or location. You can align work flow to specific immediate and future customer needs. And, you can look at the Zoo performance chain through the 4 Lens Profile.

To 'see the whole' performance chain and 'mine the meaningful' or opportunities for improvement, speed, predictability, flexibility, and leverage deserve your consideration. Using them you can profile an organization, stripping away any functional or other natural biases. And you can layer them, as you move from the broad view, into specific operations. The goal is to get to the root cause of business performance challenges and the best opportunities for improvement by studying these measures of performance together. The four lenses again are: (cheetah) speed, (elephant) predictability, (coyote) flexibility, and (ant) leverage.

Performance Chain Lenses

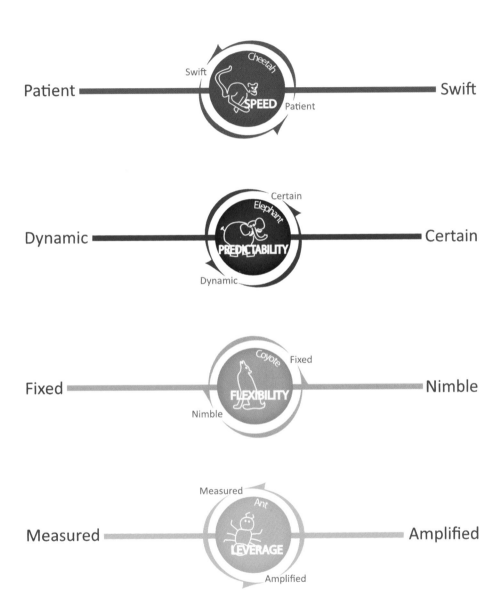

Whether a local business where the entire operation is under one roof, a business with regional or national tentacles to parts of its operation, or a truly global business with aspects of demand and supply crossing political borders, geography, languages and time zones, or a zoo, the same approach to evaluating the performance chain works in aligning better business outcomes to customer demand.

I had the opportunity to sit down with the San Diego Zoo Director, John Dunlap for an interview and do just that. John came to the Zoo with his performance orientation and Six Sigma Black Belt training from his experiences in the hospitality industry. In the interview summary that follows this chapter, John shares how he assessed the Zoo performance chain during his first visit. Then he shares how, with his team, the Zoo has been systematically upgrading their performance and customer experience over time. Speed, predictability, flexibility, and leverage all play a part in the story.

Turns out **Rashida Cheetah**, **Oralee Elephant**, **Ace Coyote**, and **Rickie Ant** all have significant roles to play in driving better performance. The CEO is lucky to have them on the team. We'll meet them again. But first, check out the interview with John Dunlap and then let me take you on a visit to possibly the most important place in the animal kingdom: the watering hole.

Interview with John Dunlap, Director, San Diego Zoo[10]

What brought John Dunlap to the San Diego Zoo?

John joined the Zoo in 2008. Prior to the Zoo, his career was in hospitality with the Starwood Hotel and Resorts where he developed a commitment to both quality (John is a Six Sigma Black Belt) and customer experience. He was happy in his career and not interested in a change when a recruiter encouraged John to take his family and visit the Zoo, which he did. During that initial visit and with his wife's help, he began to assess the experience. Together, they started taking notes. He could clearly see a world-class focus on animals. He also saw very clear opportunities for quality and experience improvements on the visitor side. *(John described a performance chain working in many respects and missing in others.)*

What he realized in that trip was that this incredible organization with its global brand created a singular opportunity to have a unique impact in the world.

John came away from that first visit with fifteen ideas to immediately impact the visitor experience. He collected a binder full of research and background that would form the basis of his interview materials as he went through the selection process with the CEO and board. This same background became the basis of John's initial play book when he entered as the Zoo's director. *(He did the work to 'see the whole' and then identified the 'meaningful' places to start improving the performance chain – and from there the customer experience.)*

When you meet John, it is clear within the first 3 minutes that he is a very organized thinker and action-oriented guy. He is also a team guy. John asked Christina Simmons, the Zoo's PR manager, to participate in the interview – to contrast her more than 20 years of experience at the Zoo with his 3. He made it clear throughout the discussion that, while he often drives the change, everything is done through teams that build out the concepts and implement the changes.

How John translates his operations and Six Sigma background from his previous hospitality industry experiences to the needs of the Zoo:

John has hired 2 people since he came to the Zoo to focus on process improvement: one to enhance revenue opportunities, the other for expense-side opportunities. The Zoo has also been building Lean and Six Sigma capabilities.

While the Zoo is very innovative on the animal side, they were not used to a lot of change otherwise. As John began to introduce the concepts and employees could see how positively the guests reacted, literally witnessing the validation, enthusiasm has built. Christina confirmed this and recent employee engagement surveys show the growth in team culture and engagement.

Aside: a couple Zoo staff members told me that on almost any given day you will see John out front – meeting people, engaging with visitors, acting on and demonstrating the experience himself.

Within 60 days of starting he personally worked in every area of the Zoo – learning the organization and exactly what work happens at each function, across the entire performance chain. From that experience and through his teams he has begun to build the visitor experience to match the world-class animal experience.

John's list of 15 things also required support of the board and his boss. He says they have lived up to his requests and the commitments they made when they hired him – 100%.

So what was on that list? Some examples:

- It was crazy to park your car. The lots were broken down, directions were confusing and traffic hectic.
- Poor way-finding – very confusing both in physical signage and the visitor maps
- No 'on stage' mentality amongst the staff
- Food was basic with little variety and a low service atmosphere. (Today 85% of the food and beverage options have been upgraded)
- No music – no 'atmosphere management' – no entertainment 'zones'
- The Zoo sits inside the incredible Balboa Park but there was little integration between Balboa Park and the Zoo
- The Zoo is a high profile conservation (animals, plants, resources in general) organization, but recycling and other visitor conservation efforts were limited
- Tour buses were old and dull
- Missing retail opportunities – particularly photography (in three years they have doubled this revenue)

The full list literally walks you through the Zoo performance chain from the moment a visitor arrives (demand is triggered) through the value creation (seeing and interacting with the animals, education opportunities, interactions with other guests and staff), value delivered (through the guides, the buses, the maps, the food), cash received (retail opportunities in key locations), and value extended (turning visitors into ambassadors and members).

Performance Discussion

The Zoo is a non-profit organization so the motivation is different than a for-profit organization. The Zoo is about conservation, education and recreation. It is not about return on investment to shareholders – it is about engagement of all stakeholders (donors, volunteers, members, community supporters, the city of San Diego, etc.) so they want to make personal investments in the development of the Zoo.

How have the needs and performance requirements evolved since you arrived?

"We have tackled most of the early obvious list – now we are developing and working on the next level of performance and experience improvement.

"An example we are wrestling with: 'Where does entertainment play in a conservation environment?' Certainly not everywhere but it definitely has a role.

"We are creating an entertainment vision that will be implemented over multiple years. Our first job was alignment of changes and basic facilities upgrades: paint, fixing anything that was broken, paving the parking lot, new way-finding – the Zoo is on its third map based on both guest and employee input. We now have the base from which to build a world class experience. 2016 is the 100 year anniversary of the Zoo. We are using this as an opportunity to raise capital for more improvements. One simple example – we are replacing temporary stages with permanent structures that can be used year-round."

Can you relate to how speed, predictability, flexibility, and leverage play a role in the way the Zoo operates? "Absolutely."

Start with Speed – okay, this is a great Leverage example, too.

"Perfection is the enemy of done. We need to move fast. But it is easy to get caught in over-analyzing decisions. Or letting an assumption of what is 'right' slow a process down. Example – our tour buses were in great need of repair and replacement. They were old, the paint was dull, seats were torn, and they run on gasoline. The assumption was that we needed to upgrade to electric buses – and we had been studying the options, literally for decades. The reality is that we could buy and replace ONE bus for $1 million, or we could spend $100,000 per bus to upgrade our current fleet – making them 'cool' to ride in and more gasoline efficient. I just put the question to our team: what kind of conservation are we deciding on? In fact it turns out it was 'greener' to reuse our gasoline buses than to purchase new electric ones. The new V8 engines are more gas efficient than the old V12 engines. We also need capital conservation. Within a few months, the team developed a plan and we began upgrading. We now have most of our buses converted and all will be done by March of 2013. Ten for the price of one. They are colorful, comfortable, cool – the kids love them, and more energy efficient. Everybody benefits. This is a Lean approach: How do you stretch your capital for most advantage and do it as quickly as possible?"

What about Predictability?

"Predictability affects us a couple ways. It can mask opportunity. It absolutely does, and yet you need it. Customers need to know what to expect. We have lots of daily reports, and check the quality of every aspect of our business. We have good or very good scores. This can make it eerily slow to change. Because we have good scores, why is there a need to change or upgrade? So we have to get underneath and understand the performance improvement opportunities and implement them in a way consistent with who we are, and bring the experience level up.

"Predictable behavior can actually pull us off our strategy. Another example: We rely on donations for much of our capital improvements. It is a classic non-profit model: a donor makes a large pledge tied to something they personally are interested in. The donation requirements may actually disrupt our performance chain. But we don't want to – or can't afford to – pass on the donation. In one very real example, our job was to 'think in the context of our long-term strategy'– not just leap at the donation and begin implementing. We used our strategic context and were able to reset the pledge with the donor. This puts the investment to better use because it fits into the overall plan we are pursuing."

And Flexibility?

"Flexibility is what extends the strategic view. You can't anticipate everything you will run into so you need the people, process and skills to adapt when the unexpected happens. Probably our most visible recent example: We had a fire at 2 AM, I'm standing watching one of our highest revenue retail outlets (our panda store) burn to the ground. While the Fire Marshall and team did their work, we went to work. By 3 AM we were already planning our recovery. By 5 AM we had one of our best contractor partners on site and within 24 hours from the fire, after the fire department released the site to us, we had the remains of the burned building completely gone and a base for a new temporary store established.

"One of our Zoo architects and I searched our resources and online to find a simple, temporary solution that we could build out quickly. We found a design that could work, started with a small structure we had that we could repurpose, and built a temporary store. This gives us time to plan the permanent building. So the timeline was:

Monday: Fire
Tuesday: Removal
Wednesday: Reconstruct temporary store
Friday: Restocked and open for business

"Our employees have to squeegee water out of the facility when it rains and everything is on carts so it has to be assembled every day. But they don't mind. They understand that this is an important part of the Zoo. It is important to our guests. Had we not acted quickly, they may have been laid off. They are making the store work and our revenue from this location is back up to nearly where it was.

"You can't make these flexible kinds of actions happen if you don't have the culture and relationships in place to make things happen immediately when a crisis or opportunity occurs. These characteristics have to be built into your performance chain long before any event."

In performance chain work there is a need for balance. As examples, all speed without predictability is not a good thing. Too much flexibility typically impacts quality and speed. How are these (or other) performance requirements balanced in the way the Zoo operates today?

"I always come down on the side of the customer: what balance is right for the experience we are building."

What are the performance priorities you are currently focused on?

"We are considered 'at the top' of our field. There is always a risk in that position – to be the best and continue to improve.

"It takes a lot of money to execute our mission, for conservation and for the guest education and recreation experience. For example: Kids are free in October. Raising money is always part of what we need to do.

"Also we have lots of stakeholders: members, donors, daily visitors, employees. They all want a great environment. The welfare of our animals is a first priority. And then using the environment to make a guest experience interesting and to unify of all the various stakeholder interests.

"We are also developing customer experience metrics. They are incredible tools, dashboards about the customer experience for every aspect of our business so we can understand customer needs and what customers want. Using this information is empowering our people to understand how they contribute to the performance chain through their individual job and how they directly impact the entire experience.

"Our job is to inspire and each role can do this. If we miss we throw off the guest.

"One example – I saw a newspaper article that said 'going to the Zoo used to be fun.' It was all about our messaging: as you went through the Zoo the reporter pointed out that everything was preachy and negative. 'Endangered!' 'At risk.' 'Don't!' The cumulative effect of all the warnings was negative.

"We've really been working on this – we can still teach and inform but do it differently. We've created Discovery Days, Jungle Bells, Mommy Meet-ups, and enhanced the Nighttime Zoo, examples of experiences that inspire guests to care and enjoy learning about the conservation efforts."

In business assessments there are tangible and intangible characteristics that drive performance. As you think about the Zoo – the tangible (to the visitor) characteristics seem obvious. What intangible characteristics of the organization are fundamental to the overall performance against the mission?

"Well, the intangible starts with why people visit. Yes, it may be about the animals – but often – it's just an opportunity for a dad or mom to connect with their kids. They want us to help them build relationships. The interactions and ways we help guests experience a 'great time' may be as important as any other aspect of the Zoo." *(Start with the problem to be solved not the product offered!)*

Who are your customers?

"Members, casual paid visitors, non-paid – such as school groups"

If I met a group of your most loyal long-term members today, what would they say most differentiates the San Diego Zoo?

"Our leadership in conservation – there are no others with our track record or willingness to step up – with all the risks – and say "we are going to save this species." So many examples: Elephants, Pandas, the California Condors..."

Wrapping up, what is a favorite Zoo story of yours that you like to share with others?

John: "In an environment like this, with all these moving parts – talk about a performance chain! We are tested with unpredictable challenges every day. And we take them on: bringing the California Condors back from the brink of extinction – we were down to less than two dozen, now we're up to 394 (as of October 30, 2011) and growing – people said it couldn't be done. Or a more recent story you saw in the news, we rescued and rehabilitated confiscated elephants from Texas that are now residing in another zoo.

"Also I need to say – we have great relationships. The city of San Diego and the people of San Diego love us. And all our partnerships that make it possible for us to do what we do."

Christina: "We have new employee orientation coming up. Probably 20 or 25 will be in the class. If they are typical of our usual new groups, only 4 or 5 will leave the Zoo, ever, for the rest of their career.

"Two days after 9/11, we had a real, credible threat and were told to evacuate the Zoo. Our employees were very supportive of getting everyone out – but wouldn't leave themselves. They wanted to stay with the animals."

Nomads of Maasai-land, Kenya, by Greg du Toit

Chapter 2
Demand

All animals require water to survive. Thirst is the common need. And the watering hole as a metaphor for a market supplies all: the weak and the strong; the slow and the fast; predators and prey. The animals all come, jostle for position, some drinking out of the footprints of others. Still others are disrupting the equilibrium with their very arrival. Each one finding a spot at the water's edge that can satisfy them, fulfilling their need.

The watering hole is no different from any marketplace where customers, competitors, vendors, community organizers, and others come take a position, vie for attention, buy and sell wares. And a business marketplace can be just as dangerous as any watering hole. On 'Black Friday' after Thanksgiving, consumers have literally been trampled to death as mobs compete at retail locations for limited items on sale in the wee hours of the morning. Companies rise and fall as newer, faster, stronger alternatives arrive. Vendors and suppliers become extinct if they can't keep up with social and technological changes. Markets, like watering holes, are critical, necessary, demanding, and dangerous places. That's what makes them exciting.

Designing a performance chain in the first instance, often long before a specific need is identified, requires understanding of the customer (animals in this instance) their need to be solved (quenching their thirst) and the market dynamics (other animals at the water's edge, for example.) Modifying a performance chain as market circumstances change and evolve requires a deep understanding of the situation and is helped by a unique perspective. Viewing the dynamics of any market, any watering hole, is best done with an expert guide. Let me show you what I mean.

Meet Greg du Toit. Greg is a wildlife photographer, eighth generation South African, and an incredibly determined human being who chose to live at (actually in) an African watering hole for months pursuing his quest for a

Photo: Greg du Toit

shot of lions drinking. During that time, he devised his own methods to capture a unique perspective – including sitting in the water up to his neck with a muddy bottom for a seat. There he sat with, as he describes it, "a frog's eye view," day after day, weeks on end – to capture a unique view of the visitors who came to the hole for a drink. Not a pleasant experience – in his own words:

"With my rear end ensconced in the muddy bottom, all that protruded above the water were my head, hands and camera. Sitting motionless in the water allowed for a detailed entomological study. I discovered that dragonfly nymphs deliver a most excruciatingly painful bite, not to mention a tiny green midge of unknown description, which is particularly partial to human flesh. The whirly-gig beetles seemed to enjoy swimming along my skin and up my legs!"

Day after day the animals came, zebra, Egyptian geese, waterbuck and warthogs, bushbuck and baboons.

"The amount of unseen life that existed and survived on that one small patch of water astounded me, and having a frog's eye view of the world gave me a completely new sense of awe for the wonderful creatures that inhabit our splendid continent," says Greg.

Still no lions. Until one day, eight months into his quest, as he looked up, along came two beautiful lionesses making their way towards the watering hole. He was about to get what he had been waiting for – and he was terrified!

"To see the two lionesses five meters away," he recalls, "I noticed their piercing yellow eyes and their bulging muscles, which seemed to tower above me. Had I been standing, my knees would have been knocking! This was it, I thought: eight months of literal blood, sweat and tears and now finally, my chance to 'get it right'."

Visit Greg's website[11] to see his amazing photos and his ability to capture the wildlife at this market known as the watering hole. Read Greg's full personal account including what drives him to such lengths in his passion to share the endangered lion population of Kenya with the world.[12]

This is an amazing story but why tell it in a business book about strengthening performance chains? Well, it is actually a perfect story of demand. Yes, for the product (water in this case) and all the other requirements impacted by the market (watering hole) environment.

And performance chains, as we defined in Chapter 1, go into motion the moment demand is triggered.

Identifying demand that you can fulfill successfully, and collecting the rewards (profit, market share, etc.) that go with it, requires as vivid a picture of the marketplace and the customers as the watering hole and animals in Greg's photographs. Without that clarity you will make mistakes in the way you design and execute your performance chain.

Marketers and customer experience aficionados (including me!) often present this pristine, orderly, even pretty, passionate and completely analytical view of demand. It is a theoretical view of the world. Customers are profiled. Their behaviors are studied, tracked and mapped. Images of happy, satisfied customers appear in advertisements online, on TV, in papers and magazines. They talk to us on the radio. Many of us know and love our customers personally, and we see them through rose-colored glasses. They have a need. We have the right product or service to help them.

Markets are defined on X & Y axes and look so completely orderly and logical. They are sized, measured, quantified, mapped, aggregated, and divided up. Demand is calculated by product or service, by segment, and by customer set. Demand is fed into the revenue lines of a company financial spreadsheet, and it all looks so beautiful and symmetrical and predictable.

This is great and valuable work and a basis for understanding demand. It is also not real and cannot be taken as fact without considering other dynamics that aren't always perfectly knowable. Customers and markets always have a way of surprising us. We need to assume some room for surprises in creating or adapting our performance chain.

Step away from that analytical and orderly image of demand (customers and prospects) and into the real world and into the center of a performance chain. Now what do you see? Demand appears fickle at the best of times. Sometimes it is overly aggressive and at other times it seems to evaporate without reason. Those sweet, beautiful customers from the advertisements turn into seeming monsters, vile, unhappy, and unable to be satisfied. That beautiful marketplace is smelly and dirty and congested with lots of other complicating factors – like competitors who like to introduce new products and services and just generally mess up the place. Oh, and then come the government regulators and the technologists to stir up the waters even more.

In other words, customers behave much as the visitors to the watering hole. And markets can be very much like the watering hole – crowded, pungent, changing with the seasons, at times very unfriendly.

We can't with complete certainty know when customers will show up. Remember it took months for the lionesses to appear. We can't always anticipate their nature. The baboons made life for Greg and others not only smelly, but disgusting and miserable. Some customers are disruptive and demanding. When the bull elephants arrive, everyone steps out of the way. It may not just be a drink of water some visitors are after. The warthogs wanted a bath. Others were checking out the food options. Demand isn't always simple to define and interpret.

All of this variability, at the customer level and the market level, needs to be factored into the decisions we make about our performance chain. As a trained observer of the watering hole, Greg did this. Let's not miss that for his purposes, Greg needed his own performance chain. Greg made the right decisions about speed, predictability, flexibility, and leverage for his objectives.

If he had been in a rush (too much speed built into his processes) he'd have missed the lions altogether and maybe countless other photographs. He chose patience over swiftness.

If he had been bound by the typical rules of a human photographer being upright and dry – the predictable way we might think about his role – he would never have implemented a strategy that found him at 'frog's eye level' – submerged and therefore able to relate to the watering hole population in a unique way. And yet, once he settled on his view, he was predictable – never letting the smell or the bites or fear get the best of him. Certainty set in as Greg understood what was working.

He started out nimbly, dynamically working the angles at the watering hole, but once he discovered what worked, his basic position was set. 'Seated on the muddy bottom,' his position became fixed and all of his flexibility came from his ability to adapt to the arriving animals with his head, hands and camera just above the water line.

Finally, Greg leveraged everything he could: making himself incognito; extending the use of time and patience (far beyond what 99.99% of the human population would have endured!); using his physical strength and presence of mind to keep himself alert and ready for the moments when the animals arrived. With mud as his foundation and water as a camouflage, Greg amplified every human and physical environmental asset to his advantage.

Like solid demand and marketplace research, through Greg's pictures and stories he is able to share with us all the elements at work at the watering hole. We can understand the customers (animals); their needs (thirst and some degree of safety); the product solution (water); and competition (other animals near the water). Greg understood the nature of the customers and their demand. It wasn't just about water. Water created the opportunity. It was the central product all were after. Timing, access, availability, coexisting neighbors, and managing danger were all factors to consider in whether any of the animals were going to get to water and satisfy their thirst.

This book assumes you've picked your watering hole and your desired role whether you've been in business a long time or are just getting started. As we go on to discuss the four performance chain lenses in more detail, the assumption is that you understand your customers, their needs and how those needs play out in the marketplace. Strong performance in your chosen marketplace requires both a fit with the external characteristics and alignment of your internal performance chain. Given that, we need to accept the requirement of a clear-eyed and well-defined view of:

- the marketplace,
- target customers,
- their experience requirements, and
- how customer needs translate into profitable demand potential for your organization.

If you don't have this foundational understanding, you need to get it and then refresh it as you go. Every interview in this book talks about the need to stay at least current with, and ideally ahead, of the market. You do this as Greg did, using customer input, actions and behaviors as guides to performance chain decisions.

The watering hole overflows in some seasons and dries up in others. As changes occur, the animals adjust to solve their need for water. Markets evolve as customer needs change and as products and services flood in or disappear. In all cases demand evolves, fluctuates and sometimes ends or is replaced as these changes occur. These changes can be slow and evolutionary or sudden and unexpected.

Building a performance chain with the capability and nimbleness to adjust as the market moves and changes can be difficult and expensive. Investments in facilities, equipment, people, and technologies can hold a company back or enable it to scale. Designing a performance chain in the first instance is a challenge. Remodeling it time and again as markets change and demand shifts can be difficult, if not downright painful and costly. A decision you make today can lock your organization into a set design for years. Precisely because we know demand fluctuates and evolves, we need ways to translate what we understand into what we do. This affects literally every part of an entire organization. The challenge is: how to create a system that allows demand to flow in, through, and out successfully fulfilled?

Demand is triggered where your customer experience begins and your performance chain goes into motion. First year marketing students learn this. Executives and front line sales people know this. And yet so often, in the functional design, we skip alignment of capabilities with customer needs and go right into product design, production and distribution. We focus, using the watering hole example, on production of the water, minimizing or ignoring all the other demand characteristics. Whether spoken or not, the logic that plays out across the performance chain is 'if we produce it, they will buy it.' Or 'we know what our customers need more than they do.' Or 'This is the way we do it here, so they'll just have to accept it.' Or 'we have this investment, we have to use it.' Or 'it's sales and marketing's job to move this stuff.'

Everyone reading this book probably has at least one personal story or experience where conflicting messages from the top of organizations about growth in revenues and the need for cost containment drive demand and supply strategies further and further apart. Not grounding every decision and action across the performance chain in well-framed demand requirements pulls an organization further into functional silos where unit or individual goals may be accomplished, but the results don't add up. Demand as the driver of performance becomes dissected, even unrecognizable, depending on your role in the flow of work.

When true demand gets compartmentalized or cloudy, performance decisions fall out of alignment with external requirements. In these cases decisions get made from internal positions of arrogance or naiveté. We either assume we know the right answers – we know our customers and can speak for our customers – or assume we can shape demand by the core product or service functions and features we create. That makes for big mistakes, lots of waste, and lost opportunity. Even if the performance chain works at some level, results end up unsatisfying. Revenues grow but we lose sight of the profit needed. Or we become so focused on margin, we miss the market opportunities to pursue profitable demand in new ways. We see some performance but not enough.

Too often companies start with what they want to produce, and then go in search of the market. Some are successful with this approach – technology companies often do this: Who knew I needed a camera in my phone? For the longest time, I didn't see the value in texting. I was not a fan of the eBook – until I downloaded my first one. DVRs changed television watching forever. It is true that sometimes, okay often, customers need help understanding what they need and want. The companies that do this well – name your favorites – do this by understanding not just the technical function or feature, but how the customer or user will adapt their lifestyle and habits to the new opportunities. These companies lead with product enhancements but really understand customer behavior. They pay a tremendous amount of attention to how their products are being used and what customers are asking for as they develop enhancements, upgrades and new offerings.

Most companies, however, are not as successful as they could be taking this product or service driven approach. They get enamored with producing the 'thing' and lose sight of all the other demand characteristics that are required in production, servicing, sale and use of the thing. They probably pay too much for development of functions and features that customers don't value and won't pay for. We all know stories of wildly overbuilt products, too costly for the problem they solve. Do you use every feature on that fancy coffee pot in your kitchen? Can you honestly use every function on that conference phone in your office? Have you ever really tried all those features built into your credit or debit card? How many of you default to calling the help line for service and listen to endless messages about trying self-help at a company's overbuilt and confounding website while waiting for assistance? We, as customers buy overbuilt and underutilized products and services all the time. As business people, we unfortunately create and perpetuate performance chains that reinforce and absorb this waste unnecessarily.

Look around your own performance chain and ask yourself a couple questions:

- How many things that are happening in your performance chain have become overly complicated and detached from your customers' true needs?
- What are we doing across our performance chain that is important to us, but customers do not value?

We underestimate the complexity of the demand beyond the core product or service or try to overcompensate by adding in more pizzazz instead of understanding the basic use requirements. Or we layer in – you've heard it – "value added" features or services. Most often these add-ons increase the cost and are seldom captured in the price. Why? Because they are our internal answers to a demand challenge, not grounded in the customer's value set.

When this happens, the performance chain that is designed can imprison the company and restrict ability to pursue even clear opportunities. These past decisions, disconnected from true demand requirements, lock the organization into further assumptions about what can or cannot be changed. Over time, instead of moving closer to fulfilling demand more productively, companies layer in additional products and services, process steps, capital investments, channels, service components and people, more costs, until the burden forces a complete redesign.

It doesn't have to be this way. It is possible to do both: serve customers by improving their experiences AND improve the overall performance of the organization. It is possible to do this without over – or under – building. Setting up a performance chain – or realigning a performance chain to the attributes of true demand – is the starting place.

Again, ask yourself:

How aligned is your current performance chain to true demand in your market? Do you know the answer – or think you know the answer?

If you are not sure, it would be worth finding out!

Greg was not at the watering hole as a customer or supplier. He was there observing. And yet, through his understanding of this environment and his keen eye, we see an example of how a balanced performance chain can work. He started with a mix of knowledge and instinct. He adapted as he learned what worked at the watering hole. He wouldn't have characterized what he did as a fine balance of speed, predictability, flexibility, and leverage, but that (and sheer guts and talent!) is exactly what he created, a performance chain that worked for his objectives.

Greg had an advantage we, in business, often do not get: he had total access to both the demand and supply requirements at the watering hole. The entire marketplace was visible to him. Many species of animals entered thirsty and left fulfilled. They returned on other days, adjusting their behaviors based on who else was at the pond. Greg could also adjust his view and actions based on who showed up. Demand was triggered and value was created and delivered dynamically – right before his camera lens.

In Chapter 1 I talked about 'Seeing the whole and mining the meaningful.' At the watering hole Greg did this from his 'frog's eye view.'

In businesses we too often take the view apart – seeing the pieces but seldom the whole. It is common for companies to think of demand and supply completely separately – to view performance in two halves. This creates the classic left hand/right hand disconnect: 'Sam, you worry about the right hand (revenue) and Sara, you worry about the left (supply)'. In this world, what do Sam and Sara talk about most? Problems. Problems created when Sam's customers are upset about some product or service failure. Problems created when Sara's production is disrupted by erratic and unexpected sales requests. Instead of demand moving in and through, it becomes a hot potato passed from one part of the organization to the next, with problem resolution adjustments along the way.

This bisection into demand and supply starts the process of moving much of the organization away from the customer need and true demand and into functional views of roles and responsibilities. Demand becomes a production headache instead of the purpose of performance. You've heard it, 'if only we didn't have those pesky customers!' Or, "our customers don't know what they need!"

How many times have you walked into a store having a sale on merchandise that nobody wants – at any price? Conversely, have you ever stood in line at a store that advertised something and lots of customers show up to buy, only to find out the item is not available? It is not a pretty sight! I've walked into plants with partially completed products (work in process or WIP) that will never make it to final production and sale because the operation was building ahead, not informed of or attuned to a change in demand. I've been on customer calls explaining why something – completely reasonable – can't be done because of some internal policy, not a capability gap. I have listened to the 'no you can't' or 'you'll have to' commands of customer service representative who don't have the visibility, authority or creativity to solve a relatively minor service delivery problem. I have heard functional leaders make decisions that will impact the company for years based on current technology enablers (or the latest cool widget) completely disconnected from an alignment between customer need and company performance.

Gaps in the performance chain decision making, such as the examples above, increase in complexity as organizations get larger and more distributed. The separation is magnified when some of the production and servicing or fulfillment is executed in multiple locations, maybe contracted to other companies in different time zones and cultures where they have zero visibility to the end customer demand requirements and know only what is in their performance contract. These outsourcing or distributed function decisions may make great sense from an operational or productivity standpoint. They can be extremely positive if, and as long as, the flows of demand in, through and out remain transparent and connected.

If, however, as so often happens, these supply and production decisions create separations and disconnects in the value creation process, demand will get blurry, modified, adjusted, or permanently altered. Customer needs get forgotten altogether. What started out as that logical, symmetrical, beautifully coherent picture of revenue opportunity becomes fractured and difficult. The more hand-offs impact the ability to understand how demand is flowing through the entire chain, the more problems will be created. Inventories will grow. Wait times and production mismatches will increase. Service complaints will rise. And revenue and profits will suffer.

As individual departments or business units focus on their narrow accountabilities, demand understanding and the triggering needs that initiate demand are lost. When that happens, future disconnects are inevitable. The further parts of the organization are removed from demand understanding, the more likely supply, fulfillment and customer satisfaction issues will grow.

We do this to ourselves and our employees. We do this to our customers by losing focus on their needs and demand as it moves across our performance chains.

We can also fix this! We have the opportunities to be like Greg, adapting our performance chain as we observe the activity at the watering hole.

Instead of viewing performance functionally, we need to look across the chain as demand is triggered, value created and delivered, payments are received and processed and new demand evolves. From a performance chain view at the highest level, demand is the first 'in.'

Remember, a performance chain is really just a system of moving pieces. It's about flow. Everything has an in and an out. Demand has flowed in. Now it needs to flow through.

Along the way, as demand moves through each work zone or process, it will transform and move out to the next one until it is transformed into a product or service that fulfills a customer need. Also along the way you create an experience that wraps your performance chain inextricably around your customers. The experience you create will either make you money or cost you money.

Viewing a performance chain horizontally or riding along with demand as it moves across a company requires a return to our friends from chapter one: **Rashida Cheetah**, **Oralee Elephant**, **Ace Coyote**, and **Rickie Ant**.

Introducing the 4 Lenses

As we leave the watering hole story and head into deeper understanding of performance chains, demand has flowed in. Now it is time to move it through and out: to create and deliver value, get paid and open up opportunities for continued growth and prosperity.

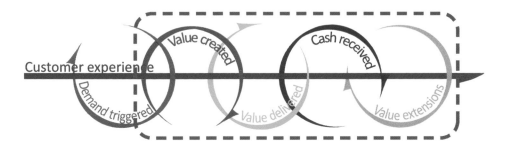

In the next chapters we will look at this overall performance challenge through the four lenses of speed, predictability, flexibility, and leverage.

We will examine:

Speed – referring to how quickly value is created and captured horizontally – across the entire chain, and vertically – in individual functions.

Predictability – asking how consistent or inconsistent is an organization in driving value – both to the customer and the company? This is an evaluation of routine, process consistency and output quality.

Flexibility – where the ability of the business to adapt to changing requirements and conditions is put to the test. As customer needs and demands shift, and new tools, materials and capabilities become available, how quickly can the organization adapt for the benefit of both customers and the company?

Leverage – which is about making or producing more value with existing resources (people, processes, technologies, physical assets) and/or making the compelling case to add resources if the overall performance improvement translates to real value created and captured.

It is time to reconnect with our characters from page one.

Cheetah Gaze, Botswana, by Dianne Ekberg Arnold [13]

Chapter 3
Speed

Rashida Cheetah races back to the shop from the meeting with the CEO. When he gets there, he's hot and tired, tail dragging. He is one frustrated cat. Like most organizations, when performance isn't where it needs to be, speed and the need for more of 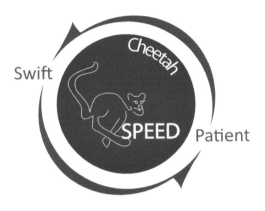 it becomes the target. But is more speed really the only or best answer?

Looking around he sees the others running fast, but things just aren't adding up. What is the problem? The boss is right. Even though everyone is busy, performance is just not where it should be – and Cheetah has vowed that he will find the answer. Heading out to the floor, he decides a quick lap around the operation will clear his head.

Designed for speed: The cheetah

Cheetahs have a unique body structure that is built for efficiency and speed. They have a smaller skull size, large nostrils to allow for maximum air intake to the lungs, and slim body structure – compact with limbs designed for a literal explosion of speed up to 70 MPH! Even the foot pads and the way the toes are set contribute to their speed. The tail is streamlined, yet designed to control balance at high speeds. Built for speed, cheetahs are very thin and, therefore, fragile. A cut in a footpad or broken toe that won't heal can be life threatening. Unlike other more muscular cats and other predators, cheetah cannot attack and drop a prey. Most often they must trip or run their prey off balance so the animal falls. When stunned and on the ground, the cheetah can attack.

Cheetah often expend so much energy while speeding along to catch prey, they overheat and must cool down before they can enjoy their kill. This is a vulnerable time for them when larger or more aggressive predators like lions or hyenas move in to steal the meal. If another animal touches a cheetah kill, the cheetah will not fight but instead moves on to run down another prospect.

Young cheetahs race with abandon – using up all their energy in speed during the chase. More mature cheetahs learn how to conserve energy and minimize the chase requirements. These more experienced cats learn how to balance their innate speed capability with the requirements of their hunt. Just because they can go fast doesn't always mean it is their best strategy.

So what can a business learn from a cheetah about applying speed to an opportunity?

Design for speed

The first place to start is in the basic design of your operations. Like the cheetah, is your organization designed for speed? If it was originally, have decisions over time made it more capable of increasing velocity or less? Whether the operation is a factory floor, an outsourced supply chain, or a call or service center, the first thing to consider is what contributes to driving speed and what gets in the way. If speed – the ability to move processes, production and fulfillment along at increasing rates – is essential to your value proposition and competitive strength, then understanding whether you're actually designed for speed is the place to start.

As a consultant working with companies across virtually every industry for the past decade, I've seen brand new buildings that constrict flow. I've seen machines worth millions sitting idle behind machines worth thousands because the process flow has the sequence out of order – or not enough of the lower cost equipment is available to fill and keep the expensive equipment running. I've seen call centers and back office operations that make business decisions to work in calendar order – or some other order – without regard to the content of the work. Rather than a clear path to move simple or low value transactions separately from complex or high value orders, the high value orders are stuck behind a raft of small transactions. Or one complex transaction bogs down the processing of all others. Speed slows down and "days revenues outstanding" (DRO) mounts. DRO is simply the time period from the moment work is completed until you have cash in the bank. If DRO extends you have an immediate and direct negative impact on your working capital. Cash you should have in the bank is not available to you – even though you have done the work and deserve to get paid.

Why does this happen? It is not because people want to mess up the drive for increased speed. It happens because a business decision is made to solve a localized problem without looking up or down stream to see what is backing up. These decisions can seem simple or benign enough, like where to locate a piece of equipment, or what sequence is easiest from an individual job standpoint. Sometimes a desire for standardization or some other corporate mandate doesn't consider physical differences in the field.

It also happens because people become used to the set up or work rules as they exist and don't question the impact on overall speed – or they literally cannot see it. Or worse, they do suggest improvements and get in trouble for challenging someone else's setup.

Sometimes the design needs simple adjustments – call those glass bottlenecks – easy to break through and fix. Nothing is inherently broken. Other times, because of the expense associated with the fix in capital, manpower, or time, the design is harder to change. Call those iron bottlenecks. Glass can easily be changed and an increase in speed can immediately start paying dividends. Iron needs a clear business case demonstrating that more speed will recover the costs of the investments.

A design for speed may have existed at one point. Then, over time, as decisions are made and implemented, these often small adjustments start to add up to bottlenecks and sluggish performance. Like the cheetah with a sore paw, the operation just won't run as fast as is otherwise possible. Cycle times get longer. Time to market suffers.

Cash receipts slow.

Overuse of speed

Have you ever been inside an organization that suffers from excessive exception handling? We've seen them in the high double digits – 40 plus percent. That's not really 'exception' – the exception has become the routine. Often those exceptions are created by fast but not precise operations. The precision problems in these cases are often caused because units of production are valued over quality or accuracy.

Or an operation is designed for one kind of speed and is being used for production that was never intended. I once worked in a media company with a beautiful, top of the line, state-of-the-art production facility. One of the best and fastest in the nation. We used to say we could produce 700,000 of one standard product every day. Ask us to produce one product at 400,000 and 2 others at 50,000 and the challenge would bring us to our knees. Include a requirement to insert a non-standard item into the core product and guess what happened? Hand inserting by hundreds of employee extras. Our beautiful, fancy, fast equipment was not designed for exceptions. So we'd race through production and then hand touch every single piece. Ouch. Over time, speeding through production and adjusting at the back end this way becomes a very expensive mismatch to the intended or desired outcome.

Maybe you are looking at warehouses of finished goods that aren't moving or work in process (WIP) that is getting stale in the corner. Building ahead of demand or storing inventory to accommodate erratic demand can be a good idea, but most often it ends up to be an expensive one. You end up building or holding stuff – finished and not – with limited and declining value. Just because you could produce it doesn't mean you should have.

Like the young cheetah overfull of energy, some operation races ahead – then tired, overworked, or lacking real demand – stops to cool down. If you're spending a lot of process time on rework and corrections or off-loading excess product on eBay or another marketplace site, chances are you have not calibrated your speed to the real level of demand you are experiencing. As the young cheetahs soon learn, just because you can run fast or process that much that quickly doesn't mean you need to work that hard. If you do, you create a buildup of materials and goods that customers don't want. Running because you can is a waste of resources that impacts the chain and overall performance negatively.

These same dynamics can show up in service organizations. We've seen call centers or sales fulfillment centers incentivized to answer calls so quickly and get off calls with customers just as quickly that they invariably leave money on the table. Between the requirements to answer all calls in seconds and limit call interactions to a minute or two, there is no listening; there is only processing of the call activity and growing customer dissatisfaction.

Many organizations become speed junkies. They often are in markets that produce and introduce new technologies at an ever faster and faster pace. In service organizations, transactions that used to process in weeks now often take days or even minutes. Continually pushing velocity up or cycle times down as demand moves through the system can bring organizations to the breaking point unnecessarily.

Or if not the entire organization, key functions start to break because they can't keep up. They become that sore cheetah paw – or serious bottlenecks. Recovery or recalibrating them can be costly.

Aligning the rate of production speed to market requirements is a continual process. Sometimes faster, sometimes slower. Competition can push an organization to drive processes and outputs up at ever increasing rates. Sometimes this is necessary but not always. Speed that is not counterbalanced with predictability, flexibility and leverage considerations becomes a burden without the necessary full value return. A good indicator that you're pushing speed at the expense of an overall effective performance chain will show up in breakage, excess rework, disconnects in the chain, cost challenges, and bad customer experiences. Looking around you will see a build of inventory – both work in process (WIP) and finished goods.

Underuse of speed

Is it worth even commenting on going too slow? Surely everyone knows you can go slow but the pressure is to go fast. Well, not always. You see slowdowns happening in a supply chain that has become disconnected. Units of operation are penalized for too much inventory at the end of a quarter, so what do they do? S-l-o-w w-a-y d-o-w-n. You see slowdowns in accounts payable when you're trying to manage cash or when the pulls (purchase orders) on a demand schedule are adjusted out. Both acts likely affect an outside supplier(s) who then must react. Their reaction may be to shift capacity to someone else. Getting the flow of services or materials back up to speed when you're ready may not match their adjusted capacity. Likely the internal teams making these decisions have no visibility to the impact of their actions on other parts of the business. From their seat, they were doing exactly what they needed to do to manage cash flow or reporting requirements.

Opposite of the problem above, one business we encountered (and I doubt they are unique) with mounting customer experience problems and a falloff in demand had traded speed for labor cost. The call center operations, tasked with saving money, calculated the lost customer impact of increasing wait times. They somehow decided customers would tolerate wait times of – get this – up to 20 minutes. This was a business-to-business service operation. This was a bad speed decision. Would you wait 20 minutes just to have the phone answered to initiate a service call (that you would later be charged for) while you were already incurring down time from whatever the problem was? Neither would their customers. Trading off speed for short-term labor savings was a bad deal. The customers knew it, and the company lost.

Again, why do these things happen? The examples above are very different but they stem from the same kinds of decisions or performance pressures. Disconnected actions or decisions are undertaken to solve a localized problem, goal or requirement. Key functions inside the organization have little or no understanding of customer requirements. Actions by separated units or functions along the performance chain create impacts they cannot see and for which they are not accountable. The overall loss in performance by idling down one operation pushes the problems downstream – or worse, introduces new problems in the rest of the chain. In the end, when the problem reaches the customer, which it invariably does, the cost is measurable in customers and revenue lost.

Speed as your friend

Now that we've looked at the potential downsides of poorly calibrated or designed speed, let's talk about the more fun upside: speed as your friend.

We all like to go fast, don't we? It is way more fun than plodding along. Speed can be a core capability that distinguishes your organization from others. Speed that is well balanced across the performance chain, that is.

Speed is the cheetah's strength. It allows them to live an independent life. It is their security when in danger. It is their source of food. It gives them a unique position in the animal kingdom.

Speed – increasing the velocity of all core processes in your business – can do the same for your business and drive better performance.

The question becomes: What kind of speed is right for your organization? And, where does speed matter most? In production? Service delivery? Cash collection?

For example, a quick pace – swift speed – in product development could be vitally important but in actual production, consistent or patient speed is more important. Or swift speed may be far more important in service responses to product failures in the field than in any production process on the line. Maybe you need to reduce your overall cycle time. Maybe you need to get to market faster. Maybe you are great at executing your product or service functions but slow to collect payments. First you need to think about speed across the entire performance chain. Where do you need to be fast and compressing time in your processes? Where is the need for a consistent rhythm or pace essential? In what ways does a change in speed drive the most value in any of your processes? Where and what kind of bottlenecks do you see? How can velocity improve the natural flow of value in, out and through your various operations? After you answer these questions, then you can design or update your design for speed.

If more is really your challenge – more output, more throughput, getting more out with the same or fewer resources – then focusing on acceleration and increasing the speed at which you are already operating becomes the driving characteristic. You need to be on the swift end of the continuum.

On the other hand, if what you really need is consistent speed, speed that time after time produces a reliable result so there are no off-balance moments, no tripping the system or waste on the floor, then more speed isn't necessarily your focus. You have neither the space nor capacity to handle a buildup of product. Customers want the flow of services at a steady uninterrupted pace. You need reliability and a certain pace of workflow. If this description fits your business, then you need to be on the patient end of the continuum.

Assessing your need for speed

If you see the signs of speed challenges in your business – too much or too little speed, bottlenecks, waste or rising rework, unevenness in the performance along connected value streams with some units moving fast, others slow or stuck – how can you go about assessing your situation accurately and then make good decisions about speed?

Like our experienced cheetah friend, you have to know how to assess whether the conditions warrant running hard, expending the energy to catch the prey, or whether you're better off pacing yourself and using your speed capabilities at just the right moments to push you to success.

First you need to know how your performance chain is actually flowing. How quickly are the ins and outs and value enhancements moving through the chain? Do you have the velocity you need for the demand you have or are you wasting resources and energy pushing too hard for the output you produce?

Conduct a speed diagnostic on your own or with help

Start with what you think and then add what you know. Measure the gap and fill in the blanks through data, observation and analysis.

What you think:

- List the ways you believe things are working, or if you have them, pull out the original specs for your process design.
- Name your expectation: should a process take a day, a month, a minute or seconds?
- How much throughput are you expecting?
- How much do you need to be on course to successful performance?
- If you increase your speed, do you have demand for it?
- Are there periods or seasons where more speed matters or is a steady flow more important to your business?

Collect what you know:

- What data – hard performance information from floor systems, accounting tools or other system output – do you have?
- Be your product or service and walk the operation making initial observations to study more carefully.
- See and document what is really happening.
- Collect anecdotes – they may not be fact but they can be excellent pointers to challenges you will want to investigate more completely.

If you feel you are too close to your operation to see it clearly, get help. There are plenty of excellent resources in the market who can help you assess your situation and decide where to focus. There are also several approaches you can take and many Lean and Six Sigma tools, among others, you can use.

Here are two examples of tools that can help you diagnose your speed (and you'll later see how they can help balance speed decisions with predictability, flexibility and leverage!):

Value Stream Mapping (VSM)[14]

Yes, it has been around for a while, and yes, it is still one of the best ways to start a performance chain assessment. Value stream mapping, originating at Toyota and called "material and information flow mapping," is a Lean technique. Through the mapping process you can analyze and design the flow of materials and information required to bring a product or service to a customer. While it was born in manufacturing, it can be applied to virtually any value chain. What can a Value Stream Map (VSM) tell you about speed? Several things:

1. What your actual process times and flow are by zones of your operation.
2. Where your process actually adds value and where you have non-value-added activities. In other words, where you have long wait times, where you see work stacking up in queues, and where you have work regularly or permanently stuck in a holding pattern.
3. Where and how much you're either in line or out of line with your stated performance specs (if you have them).
4. Where, if you concentrate, you can best improve your overall

operation with a surgical focus on the areas with speed challenges.

Once you have a Value Stream Map you will have a clear view of your total cycle time and your lead times. From here you can take corrective actions to break through those constraint areas and reduce your process times.

Error Proofing

I know – seems so obvious. But remember, speed problems often show up first as errors – in production quality and in service quality. Error proofing is clearly a factor when we get to predictability but it can also help quickly align speed to quality and reduce cycle time through reduced frequency of errors and the process duration to fix them.

A few other questions you can research to decide if you need to learn more and/or make speed adjustments:

1. Do you track and have good data on actual value-add times (true process time versus all activities)?
2. Is there a method to track process, queue, wait and hold times across your performance chain?
3. Is total cycle time or lead time of any process understood, tracked and trended?
4. Do you have a work prioritization process in place that is understood and followed?
5. Do you see a lot of young cheetah behaviors – your people running around, working hard, tiring out, without the

production you would expect or need?

Improving speed – moving everything through the system as swiftly as possible or achieving a steady, maybe even patient pace – is really about aligning the velocity of all core processes to your business objectives and customer requirements.

Be like our cheetah friend and enjoy a good run!

Interview with Steve Milligan, CEO, Hitachi Global Storage Technologies (HGST) [15]

It seemed natural that an interview with the CEO of Hitachi Global Storage Technologies would best fit at the end of a chapter about speed. No other industry faces the speed and compression challenges quite the way the disc drive manufacturing world experiences those customer requirements and market pressures. As you'll soon see, however, Steve Milligan only thinks about speed in context with predictability, flexibility and leverage. He understands speed. He also understands that speed without balance and innovation doesn't get you where you need to go. So really, this is the perfect placement for this conversation.

The inside of a disc drive manufacturing plant is an amazing world. The complexity, the unbelievable engineering feats undertaken every day, the precious metals and other materials required, the machines that can execute tasks the human eye cannot see, the 900 or 1000 process steps to create a 'wafer' (just the first phase of the full product production process) boggle the mind. Somehow it all works. And as the demands for digital data storage grow with each new gadget on the market, the product specifications get more and more complex.

It should be noted that at the time of this interview, HGST is in the middle of a merger process with Western Digital. Combined, their challenges, as discussed with Steve, remain the same.

Here is how the company describes itself on its website.

Mission

We provide digital storage that delivers pioneering technology and quality that customers can count on.

The company provides a wide range of products that includes advanced hard disk drives, enterprise-class solid state drives, and innovative external storage solutions and services that store, preserve and manage the world's most valued data.

Hitachi drives are used by students and families, small-office/home-office workers, leading-edge, high-transaction enterprises and major computer, consumer electronics and automotive system manufacturers throughout the world. The Hitachi storage products integrated into these personal and business lifestyles safeguard everything from a family's personal photo legacy to critical business transactions and documentation, data-intensive, creative digital filmmaking files and hours of personal and family entertainment captured in video, music or gaming files.

Hitachi GST was formed in 2003 from the strategic merger of the storage technology businesses within IBM Corporation and Hitachi, Ltd. Since that time, the company has built on the heritage of both industry pioneers to grow profitably as a major contributor in the global storage industry. The company has worked to bring a customer-focused and full-service approach to its storage solutions. In doing so, the company has set a high standard for product and service excellence with world-class operations, substantial technical knowledge and a comprehensive customer support infrastructure.

Chances are, as a business leader and consumer, you have HGST drives in one or more of the tools you rely on every day: your PC, your phone, storage of your family and vacation photos, your GPS system...

Steve's background:

Steve has been at HGST since September of 2007, entering as the CFO. In February of 2009, he became President, and CEO at the end of that year. He came to the company with a disc drive and technology company background from Western Digital and Dell.

What drives your passion for the business?

"I think that the hard drive business, like the technology industry overall, is all about innovation and change. Being in the hard drive business requires innovation and rapid execution. It is that combination that is interesting and very challenging."

What is different today at HGST than when you started?

"Let's see, I have to put myself back in the 2007 mode. Just by way of background, in fiscal 2007, HGST lost money – $400 million. For the first 5 years of its existence it lost money and had only 4 non-sequential quarters of profitability. When I arrived in 2007, costs were out of control. We didn't have an efficient supply chain, we had limited flexibility, and we weren't even playing as a competitor in the non-commodity space.

"Starting with 4th quarter of 2007 and until today all quarters have been profitable – except 2 that occurred at the start of the initial financial markets meltdown.

"In fiscal 2010, we made over $600 million. The shift from losses to profit is about a $1 billion swing in 3 years. So a pretty dramatic change."

What changed in the business to drive this dramatic financial performance improvement?

Steve led a strategic planning effort, one of his first assignments, as the new president in 2009. Through that process he built an understanding about the business in two parts:

- The 'commodity' based business that serves a specific segment of the market (and how most of the external world sees the disc drive business); and the
- 'Non-commodity' based part of the market where technology innovation is really more relevant and a driver in all key decisions.

"On the commodity side we have to be cost competitive; we have to have a supply chain that can deliver at a fast pace that is predictable; and we need scalable technology. On the non-commodity side, product differentiation makes all the difference. You have to start with the customers and build an understanding of what they are trying to do. Then solve for that. And you have to have the flexibility to be able to see, design and execute on these new requirements quickly. Engineers can solve any challenge, as long as they have a clear understanding of the need they are solving for."

So the problem or opportunity you solve for on the non-commodity side is data storage and the shifting requirements (migration to the cloud as an example), and how you solve the need is through disk drive (storage) technology innovation.

"Exactly. Growth is in data (in the cloud). It is where we are playing AND we are now winning.

"During the planning process, we looked at our capabilities stemming from our IBM + Hitachi heritage. We believed we had the product capability we needed to compete aggressively on the non-commodity side. We also knew we were never going to be the price leader on the commodity side but we had to be in a position to be cost competitive. This orientation and six core capabilities we've been developing have driven all the change and improvement in performance."

Let's talk specifically about your performance chain and how relevant the lenses of speed, predictability, flexibility, and leverage are to your business.

"As I indicated, we are focusing on the development of six competencies that drive our business success. Speed, predictability, flexibility, and leverage need to be present in each of the six. If you think of them in a circle –as your innovation levers – sometimes you need more speed, other times more flexibility. We are constantly adjusting these four lenses, but the core requirements don't change."

Can you say more about how speed, predictability, flexibility, and leverage play a role in the way your company operates?

"The start of all of this is the market and changing conditions. Back when I entered HGST, the company did not differentiate. Today, what's happening is that the market and associated product roadmap now drive decisions. In the commodity side we design for cost – to be cost competitive. On the non-commodity side, through design innovations we can help customers see new opportunities. When we do that the competition is locked out, at least for a period until they can retool and catch up."

Can you run both commodity and non-commodity business through the same performance chain?

"We have to (run both sides through the same performance chain). It is the only way to be cost effective. And, there is enough commonality so that we can leverage our capital assets and supply chains for both.

"I think of it as a kind of a right brain/left brain thing. We have got to have the technology and we have to apply the right thinking. Engineers are built to solve problems. They can either put their brains to solving 'design at low cost,' or to solving a whiz bang challenge. But they have to know what they are trying to solve. Both can be interesting and rewarding but we have to be clear: what is the need we are solving?

"We need to optimize the core – all six key elements – of the hard drive business.

"We have to move fast.

"Commonality allows us to be flexible.

"Leverage is critical. Each one of these has a reason they are important to every aspect of our business.

"Conceptually, my view is that we spent a lot of time at the functional level across the company dealing with the interaction of all these things – speed, predictability, flexibility, and leverage."

Do you have a performance chain process in place now that you feel is well oiled or well defined?

"Yes, we have a process. I assume it is never very well oiled. You always have to worry about what you don't know and be willing to adjust. This business is always dynamic. The only time you get caught is when you think you've got it nailed. You see this in companies that change the industry and then settle in. I saw this at Dell. Dell was ahead on innovation and then got stuck in their own model. Others come in and "move the cheese." I want to be the one moving the cheese! Speed, predictability, flexibility and leverage all play a role. What you're getting at is: what is the right balance? For us it changes all the time.

"We're going through a real problem right now with the floods in Thailand. In Japan with the 2011 earthquake, we had to be nimble. We recovered faster than people expected. Always assume the unexpected will happen and be ready to act on it.

"Something happens – now you need speed – now you've got to be quick in adapting. And you've got to set the capability for speed before you need it. In this scenario, predictability and leverage are out the window for a time. Our focus has got to be to get the operation running or alternatives in place. That requires flexibility.

"You can't wait until something happens to worry about flexibility. Then it is too late. Flexibility built in is what gives you speed to recover in a situation like this.

"Balance across the performance chain is a dynamic process."

You emphasize innovation – how are you introducing innovation at HGST?

"Every business has to innovate – or you become obsolete.

"We've introduced market sensing. This is not rocket science but it is getting out and understanding what your customers are trying to do. Not what they are buying but what they are trying to do. Don't wait to see what is ordered – get out in front of them and see what will be needed.

"We are also really trying to drive a deeper level of customer engagement. The relationships in our business, like others, tends to exist with the procurement function. And that function tends to be cost-focused and shorter term focused on 'What is the next Purchase Order?'

"We are trying to drive the engagement upstream to the product people or the customer's technology people, so we can understand what they are working on and get ahead to differentiate and innovate.

"We can be cost-competitive but we are not structured to be the cost leader – so we have to find something else to differentiate. For us, that has become technology innovation – real product changes. We have also beefed up our marketing organization. More thought leadership, study of the broader storage market, drawing out the elements that really determine where the market is going to go.

"Here is an example that will sound obvious: The market is moving to thinner and lighter products. That to us translates to X,Y and Z – (width, length and height) requirements. In our industry 9.5 MM height was the standard. We saw 'thinner and lighter' and came out with a new 7 MM standard. We forced everyone in the industry to adapt to our new standard. You can put a 7 MM drive in a 9.5MM slot but not vice versa. Then when customers saw this they realized – 'oh, now I can design differently.' This positions us and and locks out our competitors and forces them to adapt."

Summing up your performance chain journey?

"We were not flexible. We were not predictable. We didn't respond in a speedy way. We had to revamp all of that. We've now progressed to the place where we are flexible, we are predictable, we have the speed we need and we are helping customers solve bigger problems and opportunities. Our customers are trying to build a better mousetrap. For those that buy only on cost, we are competitive but now our sweet spot is that we can help them with their own innovations. We are the quality leaders – we can take what a customer is doing and help them make it better. That is how we win.

"Most people say we are a commodity – again there is a big part of the market that is mature and cost-driven. We have to play there and do. But that is not the whole story."

And if I'm hearing you right – the innovations of today (on the non-commodity side of HGST) feed the commodity business and volume drivers for you tomorrow.

"Exactly."

Watering Hole Trio, Zimbabwe,, by Dianne Ekberg Arnold

Chapter 4
Predictability

Oralee Elephant takes the usual route back from the meeting to her office where she finds all the other elephants in place, doing exactly what they have learned to do and have done with absolute precision for years. She's got a terrific herd. But the discussion at the operations review is nagging at

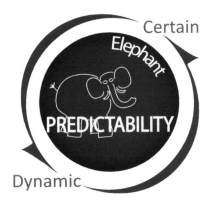

her. She looks around. She can't make sense of the disconnect between what needs to get done and what IS getting done. She's retread this same ground time and time again with the same results. This time, she vows, she will find a path to a new level of predictability that matches the company and customer needs. She calls a staff meeting.

A collective memory that drives predictability: The elephant

Elephants are amazing creatures and almost sadly, predictable to a fault. Walking the same paths based on inbred knowledge shared over generations often brings them into direct conflict with human development. The effects can be devastating. Researchers have found that if an elephant herd is in a particular spot on September 30 of one year, barring some catastrophe or environmental change (like civil war, a new village or farm, or a new commercial road cutting off their path), that same elephant herd will very likely be in the same place again on September 30 the next year and the next.

The first year of an elephant's life maps out its entire environment. It learns the water pans and migratory patterns that will govern life unless something forces a change. During the long Angola war – over 30 years – elephants (all animals) were displaced and cleared out, finding refuge in other places away from the dangerous humans. Within just a couple of years after the war ended, the elephants – even some that had been born in other locations – moved back into Angola to pick up the exact migratory patterns of their ancestors. Now that is predictability!

Herds are matriarchal and do split up from time to time. Family reunions happen, unlike most other mammals that never reconnect once they separate. When the herds meet up again, maybe after prolonged periods, they exchange formal greetings – sort of their version of shaking hands and hugs. They know each other and predictably, are happy to reunite for a visit.

Elephants produce a low frequency rumble that you and I can't hear but that travels up to 2 or 3 miles. Through this rumble they can find each other and recognize each other. Through sounds they pick up with their large ears (and now researchers are studying whether elephants pick up signals and frequencies through their feet on the ground), they gather the information they need to stay the course. Safe to proceed.

Danger ahead, advance with caution. Through a keen sense of smell, the odd scent of a human intruder on the path sends a warning. The elephants are moving ahead as planned – and constantly gathering information to guide their walk.

Predictability is grounded in known behavior. How does elephant behavior – memory – translate to business?

Let's start with the obvious: Consistency

Elephants are nothing if not consistent. Is your operation consistent? If good things happened yesterday in your operation, can you expect the same good things to happen today? If you produced 1000 widgets yesterday, can you produce at least 1000 widgets today? Assuming call volumes in your service center have peaks and valleys, are you prepared to answer each call with the same level of precision – without wasting or taxing resources? As demand grows (thinking good thoughts for your business), can you predictably adjust to fulfill it? As demand changes, can you predictably adjust to accommodate new requirements?

Consistency comes from clear operating practices, processes, well-oiled machines (in the real and metaphor sense) and consistent behaviors. Baby elephants learn consistency in their first year and then walk it the rest of their lives unless interrupted.

Consistency also must be informed by your customers. Qualitative customer input should be one barometer of whether your consistency is working for you or against you. You may have the stats but do you know the facts and opportunities underneath your good scores? Regular and meaningful discussions with customers can highlight disconnects, identify trends, and frame system performance requirements in ways that give dimension to actual data. These conversations can be done by leaders in the organization very easily or by outside resources. The trick is to not make the evaluations a series of yes/no questions and to gather input regularly, not just when there is a problem.

Businesses often fail the consistency test by falling into one of two traps:

- They tinker and modify to the point of distraction. They act more like the dogs in the movie "Up," chasing every squirrel that comes along – instead of emulating the elephant and repeating what works.
- They fall into overly rigid patterns, codified and calcified over time, too much like the memory-driven elephant, repeating old practices even when they no longer work.

For the tinkerers reading this book, you know exactly what this disease is... continuous improvement run amok. The last book an executive read instantly becomes the mantra of the day and drives change initiatives into the organization, until they read the next book (this one excepted of course). I'm a fan of new ideas, and tend toward the 'let's change' side of the world myself, but I've learned that without careful thought about the impact to consistency requirements, you can do more harm than good.

Just as with the speed junkies in the previous chapter, in the predictability realm, tool junkies can make a terrible mess. Every new technology, faster machine, hot, cool new analytical tool, etc. is viewed as 'the thing' to help drive performance. Sometimes they do. Often they are a distraction. And (previewing our leverage discussion) too often they waste capital and pull us off the true and reliable path that could have been better improved with a little common sense and information already available or easy to collect.

Consistency is also unintentionally impacted by decisions driven more from a business values set than an understanding of what drives performance. Take development of people – a noble and worthy value. Often development is implemented through a form of job rotation. This can be and often is great for development reasons. It can also cause a slip in consistency – not because the move is intended to disrupt, but because the shift creates a natural opening that causes a change. It may or may not be helpful. If job rotation becomes the end instead of the means, it can start to chip away at the performance chain in unexpected ways. If the processes and procedures – and logic – tied to customer demand are well documented and protected in the rotations, then these shifts and fresh eyes can actually help evolve consistency in a meaningful way.

Going to the other extreme can be just as bad. As with speed, consistency can be overdone. Another example, back to my media/publishing experience from the previous chapter: Before I joined the company, a new state-of-the-art printing plant had been built. Over the 125-year company history, production had shifted from the old (ancient) hot type to cold type and finally to digital presses. A Lean team of internal employees commissioned shortly after I arrived (I take no credit for their great work) discovered that in spite of the upgrades – new plant, new equipment, and new management tools – there were still hot type and cold type procedures carried out, day after day after day, years after the last hot type press had left the (old!) building. What happened to that work and effort for no value, one can only imagine. The fix was a change, but relatively easy and the benefits significant.

That may be a bit extreme, but then again, maybe not. How could such a thing happen, you might be wondering. It happened because performance through the chain was 'good enough' so no one was looking. Again, I'd like to think that was uncommon, but in my many years of consulting after that corporate experience, in every variety of company large to small, I see it over and over again.

Do you have any of what I have come to call 'trailing history' practices in your operation? My guess is you do. Do they improve your consistency of output or quality? No. Do they take up resources and cost you money? Yes. Do they in any way help your customers of today? Unlikely.

Work rules also can trap an organization into historical practices that, yes, ensure consistency of activity, but may bear no relation to the consistency required for customer benefit. These work rules certainly get imbedded in union contracts that become very difficult to change. They can as easily exist in non-union situations where job descriptions are old or processes and procedures have not been updated. Out-of-date practices get reinforced by a culture that says 'this is the way we do things here.' Again, consistency, but like the elephant trying to stay on a path that has been replaced by a highway, not the kind that is helpful.

Preparing for the "unpredictable"

Discussing the traps of too much predictability is probably the right time to bring up planning for the 'unpredictable.' As several of the interviews point out, the unpredictable happens. Floods in Thailand. Earthquakes and a nuclear disaster in Japan. A fire at 2 AM. Maybe a security breach at an airport. The collapse of a political system or economy somewhere in the world – or on a much more localized basis, the bankruptcy of a key customer or supplier. The time to establish these recovery and adaptive measures to ensure your consistency is long before you need them. Anticipating the unpredictable requires an ear to the ground and relationships in place that can be helpful in a time of need. Like the elephants sending warnings through rumblings issued miles away, you can have early warning systems and strategies in place for those unexpected events.

Quality is the centerpiece of predictability.

Quality is the reason companies work so hard to maintain performance. First, you must establish the quality levels you need in production or service delivery that tie to customer expectations, and then develop the methods and practices to repeat the execution over and over again.

The performance chain is defined in Chapter 1 as: all the tangible and intangible elements that have to move from the moment you trigger demand until you have cash in the bank; all the ins and outs that have to work together and align to your target customer experience to drive the outcomes you want.

We've probably all stayed in chain hotels that have the same footprint, the same rooms, the same beds and work stations, and yet as you move from one to the other in your business travels, you know they just are not the same. The tangible elements add up but the intangibles don't: behaviors and customs and atmosphere cannot be as easily transported from one location to another. At the other end of the spectrum you may have a favorite restaurant that you visit time and again because you just know you will love the meal and can trust the service and atmosphere on every occasion.

Some busy airports (I've been through a lot of them, probably you, too!) move people in and through, onto planes and out easily, even with all the TSA or other government regulations. Others feel like a cattle call – totally disorganized and disorienting. Same basic customer need. Same regulatory requirements. Same security challenges. And yet, some work and some don't. It is not true that the bigger they are or the busier they are, the worse they are. In fact, some of the best are the biggest and busiest. The volume of traffic moving through the performance chain in those large, busy airports actually helps drive higher standards of quality and methods for solving traveler needs by the millions every day. At www.Airliners.net various experts were asked to estimate the number of global airline passengers per day. The numbers I saw in the postings ranged from 4 – 5 million. That is a lot of individual experiences to get right – or even mostly right – in any airport on any day.

In product companies or manufacturing companies, the quality focus is often on the tangible characteristics of the product itself. That is as it should be and critically important. Particularly true if you outsource manufacturing or components of manufacturing; keeping quality standards of production in line across the entire network is essential. All the elephants in your herd need to walk the same path with the same consistency. You need your own set of 'low frequency rumbles' to keep the communications open and the processes, one unit after another, in line. You need to worry about and ensure the quality of the materials; the craftsmanship of construction; the visual appeal; the imbedded functions and features. You need to ensure that the final product actually works as specified – without a lot of waste or rework.

However, that is almost always not enough. When I have heard manufacturing or product executives complain about fickle customers, it is usually not about shifting tangible product requirements. Those, if you know your business at all, are pretty easy to solve. Not to minimize often amazing engineering feats, but for those that live and breathe product design and production, it is their expertise, it is what they do and what they love.

The quality issue often comes down to all the intangible, or sales, servicing and fulfillment, issues that surround the product. Getting a quality product out the door is one thing. Getting it to the customer as they want it, in the order they want it in, in the time frame that they want it, with the assistance or independence that they want, is the challenge.

That is why we need to think about quality across the entire performance chain before we invest in any fixes. Otherwise, you can spend precious working capital refining an already great product or service, but miss the dis-satisfiers in the process. Quality is really achieved when every function or aspect of an organization contributes to the ins and outs of the performance chain in ways that add up to solving the complete customer need.

Output is the other predictability consideration.

Maybe your quality is high, but your ability to produce is uneven. Maybe your overall production levels are fine, but movement through the chain gets stuck in spots so other areas have to make up for the backlog. Maybe your quality and production are motoring along just fine but you don't seem to have the capacity you need to handle increasing demand loads. Maybe your predictability is great when you have a steady inflow of orders but falls apart if you hit peaks and valleys. Like the elephant traveling the same path, you need signals to tell you where adjustments in your movement forward need to be made.

Cash, money in the bank, loyal customers, and growth opportunities all derive from the output you are able to reliably move through your performance chain. We've all seen 'fire fighter' organizations that in a crush can make anything happen. For a limited time they can drive output up. However, that expenditure of energy and approach is costly and short lived. Output becomes dependent on heroic acts. Like an elephant that doesn't understand why there is now a village where her path used to be and keeps running into obstacles she doesn't understand. If she cannot find a way to lead her herd around the village, the herd will likely never make it to the other side. We want elephants to survive and we want our businesses to thrive. That means managing output by solving problems along the way.

Building the predictability that works for your organization.

There is only one kind of predictability, right? Well, no. As with speed (and upcoming flexibility and leverage) you have choices based on the business you're in, your value proposition and your customer need requirements.

On a continuum, those choices may look something like this:

If you need precise quality and a consistent level of output, your business belongs on the right and all your ins and outs through your system need to be managed with certainty.

If your business allows for a lot of customization or tailoring of products or services, chances are you need predictability that is dynamic, or on the left. In this case you need to be able to quickly assimilate a range of variables and deliver back a predictable output.

Getting to the kind and level of predictability that you need.

If you want to develop a clear view of your current predictability and set your sights on certainty or dynamism, here are a few ways to get started. One is by using the same Value Stream Mapping process you read about in the speed chapter. That same guide can help reveal completeness and accuracy issues. It can also orient you to natural improvements in your production or servicing process that can increase your quality and output.

Zone Mapping

Another kind of mapping may be helpful either in addition to or instead of the VSM, depending on your needs. Call this Zone Mapping. This approach looks across an entire performance chain, detailing each in, out and move across functions and interactions with your customers. Functions are considered but it is the flow that is important, and the value added along the process flow. Zone Maps detail how demand flows in, out and through the entire process. This approach exposes eddies or rework loops that create inconsistencies and breakdowns in predictability. They also let you look across functions for the evenness of flow as demand is being served along the chain.

Error Proofing (Probably your most important predictability set of tools)

Error proofing is a basic – and powerful – approach to understanding gaps in predictability and rooting out process improvements that can materially drive up quality – most often without significant investment. Do not overlook it as a discipline or underestimate its helpfulness.

If you want to get started on better understanding your predictability needs and current performance, here are a few more questions you can research with information you probably already collect:

1. Is your actual customer delivery performance consistently equal to the committed schedule?
2. Are personnel close to the process routinely involved in root cause analysis of identified trouble spots? If so, how often are their recommendations implemented successfully?
3. Is the accuracy you deliver to customers tracked, trended and used to drive corrective actions?
4. What is your formal revision management process for implementing changes to any process or change to workflow that is intended to impact quality, consistency or output?
5. Do you have appropriate predictability metrics in place that match your need for certainty or dynamism?
6. Do you encourage training and updates on the latest tools and trends?
7. Do you have easy input opportunities for employees and customers?

Creating and reinforcing predictability drives quality and output. If you want to tame and gain the benefits of a high-functioning performance chain, internal and external processes need a consistent and repeatable path.

That rumble in the distance is likely our elephant colleague heading out for her daily walk. Join her and find out where predictability can take you in your business.

Interview with Richard Davis, Chairman, President and CEO, U.S. Bank

A confession before this interview: I am a U.S. Bank Alum (actually the predecessor organization, First Bank System, but U.S. Bank still counts me as an alumni). I left long before Richard Davis arrived. I left after a time of great upheaval at the bank. I often describe my time there as a 'fairy tale' experience. I had many career firsts and wonderful opportunities that shaped my professional career after 'the bank.' I also experienced the great swings of an organization with high-high times and low-low times. I left happy and thankful for (most) of my experiences, but many people over the years didn't leave as positively.

Around town over the past few years (U.S. Bank is headquartered in the Twin Cities, MN where I live), you don't hear about the wild swings in the bank performance or the waves of unhappy employees exiting anymore. In fact you hear the opposite. At the time of this interview, we are in the middle of an economic struggle that has the banks – all banks but mostly the big ones – painted as the villains almost daily in the news. And yet, here is U.S. Bank, the fifth largest bank in the country and their story is different: Their performance is strong and steady. They were the first large bank to repay TARP funds and did it within 8 months. They aren't in mortgage meltdown. They work with the regulators. Employees are happy and challenged and customers are positive.

What is different? I know Richard Davis would, by nature and reputation, point to others in his organization, but the bank story of consistent, impressive performance has to start with him. I was at an Alum luncheon and heard Richard speak about, among other things, predictability. Specifically he was referring to not surprising your customers or your employees. That talk prompted my request to include a conversation with him in this book.

About U.S. Bank (from their website): [16]

Minneapolis-based U.S. Bancorp (NYSE: USB), with $330 billion in assets, is the parent company of U.S. Bank National Association, the 5th largest commercial bank in the United States. The company operates 3,089 banking offices, 5,092 ATMs in 25 states, and provides a comprehensive line of banking, brokerage, insurance, investment, mortgage, trust and payment services products to consumers, businesses and institutions. U.S. Bancorp and its (62,000) employees are dedicated to improving the communities they serve, for which the company earned the 2011 Spirit of America Award, the highest honor bestowed on a company by United Way.

About Richard Davis:

Mr. Davis is Chairman, President and Chief Executive Officer of U.S. Bancorp. He has served as Chairman since December 2007, as President since October 2004 and as Chief Executive Officer since December 2006. He also served as Chief Operating Officer of U.S. Bancorp from October 2004 until December 2006. From the time of the merger of Firstar Corporation and U.S. Bancorp in February 2001 until October 2004, Mr. Davis served as Vice Chairman of U.S. Bancorp. Following the merger, Mr. Davis was responsible for Consumer Banking, including Retail Payment Solutions (card services), and he assumed additional responsibility for Commercial Banking in 2003. Mr. Davis has held management positions with our company since joining Star Banc Corporation, one of our predecessors, in 1993 as Executive Vice President.

Let's start with your passion for the business – and specifically U.S. Bank

"I could have been a pastor as easily as a banker. I started as a teller, working my way through school. I became interested in 'how does it all fit together?' I'm one of those guys – "just tell me how it works."

"My passion comes from people. It is a blessing of this job that I am in a position to help empower people.

"We are in a service business. I believe in servant leadership. One of the business books that left a lasting impression on me was Flight of the Buffalo." *(Flight of the Buffalo: Soaring to excellence, learning to let employees lead. (By James Belasco and Ralph Stayer)* [17]

Step back to when you first became CEO. (2006) What were the challenges you faced then?

"When I stepped into my role, we had disaffected employees. We are in a service business, which means we need really really engaged employees who serve and create happy customers who in turn lead to results for the bank. At the time we didn't have that.

"We held a large investor relations event about a year after I became CEO in 2007. I built my whole presentation around how employees were going to take the front seat in our business. One analyst who follows the bank, actually likes the bank, publicly questioned the approach and put me on the spot in the meeting. She was doubting that a focus on employees would have the needed impact." *(Three years later in private, that analyst told Richard he was right – focusing on employees was paying off.)*

Since that time, how have the needs and challenges evolved?

Richard is a natural story teller and in response to this question, he introduced a simple philosophy that has had a big impact: CPR, which stands for: Consistent, Predictable, and Repeatable. Three principles that drive decisions and impact all stakeholders positively.

"Every constituent love these things:

- Investors love predictability!
- Customers want all three: really they want "no surprises"
- Employees like CPR because it gives them confidence in the work they do, the decisions they make, and they like to represent it.

"The key is not to do things out of character with who we are (as an institution). It works."

We're doing this interview in an uncertain time for banks with lots of regulatory change. We read a lot of negative things about other banks, not U.S. Bank, and a lot of complaining by other bank leaders. How do you keep the organization focused in a time like this?

"Here's how I look at it and what I say about it: First we're a bank;

regulation is a fact of our lives. Second, we have 62,000 employees. I want 60,000 of them focused on customers and I want them to trust that the other 2000 are dealing appropriately with regulatory changes and have their backs. That the 2000 have the best interests of the 60,000 and our customers in mind as we react and respond to changes. *(Talk about a leverage concept as well as reinforcing predictability!)*

"I don't complain about regulators. If I do it, it gives 62,000 other employees a reason to be frustrated. My view is: Stop whining. Lead. Look for the light – the true light at the end of the tunnel. The real question we should be asking each other is "What role did you play in our economic recovery?"

If you think about your company's performance chain (or many performance chains) what key attributes come to mind?

"We are a service business. For us it is people – empowered people."

Can you relate to how speed, predictability, flexibility, and leverage play a role in the way U.S. Bank operates?

"Sure. Do you want me to talk about that now?"

Great, can we start with predictability? At the U.S. Bank alumni luncheon I heard you basically telling a predictability story. That's what prompted my request for this interview.

"Predictability, right. This goes with 'CPR.' No surprises – providing consistently good service. Communications across all levels of employees is critical. One example: We have a quarterly leader meeting with 1000 leaders. We talk about the business, the environment. We talk up to them and empower them to do the same with their employees. Rather than controlling the flow of communication as you might expect, these 1000 leaders asked that we expand the information sharing. So we're now having a similar conversation with the next 6000. The idea is to build understanding and empowerment, leader to leader. If we want consistent performance, we have to rely on each employee to act within their role with as much information as possible."

Leverage in the classic financial sense is a key function of a bank. But can you talk about leverage from a performance chain perspective?

"In our business, leverage in a performance sense is, again, all about people. I fully believe if employees are happy, empowered and know what to do, they will drive happy customers and happy customers drive results. I tell people all the time, if you like what you do, do it for the rest of your life. People like to be validated now and forever – whether they are a teller or any other job."

Do you have a customer experience definition that is well understood across the organization?

"Not really – not the way you are asking the question. We need to and definitely do set a base of being "trustful, honest and transparent." That is the basis of our customer experience. Beyond that we need each employee to be informed and able to act on the spot, and shape the customer experience.

"This is where speed and flexibility play a key role in the bank's performance chain. Having empowered employees who can act on the spot requires having the systems and processes in place to support individual employees making judgments, adapting to the information during the transaction or exchange, and being empowered to act."

If I met a group of your most loyal long-term customers today, what would they say most differentiates US Bank?

"We haven't stopped doing anything. We are consistent. They would say, 'Wow, U.S. Bank employees like what they do and they do it better than anyone else."

Do you have a last story you would like to share?

"Through the Itasca Project (a Minnesota organization that includes 50 of the largest companies in the state), I was involved with 46 CEOs in a Habitat for Humanity work day. We are all type As. When we arrived for the day, we were trained in our duties and the project rules by 26 year-olds. 26! We had a blast. At the end of the day, I asked our 26 year-old guides how we did. They said we were the best CEO group they had ever had. I asked 'Why?' They said, "You followed directions, you worked together, you followed the rules. It's really great to see that leaders can follow!"

Mousing Coyote, Yellowstone National Park, by Laurie Excell

Chapter 5
Flexibility

Ace Coyote heads back to the den. He needs time to plan. He needs to gather the others and assess the situation. He needs to think and absorb all the information from the operations discussion, but he is already making notes about things that need to change.

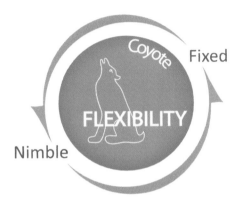

Along the return route, he doesn't have time for chit-chat so he stays out of sight – watching everyone and all the activity with new eyes. He's looking for the opportunities that can be his opening to change up the process and bring more creativity into the company. Arriving at the den he sees the young ones playing – they have no rules for how things should be done. Maybe there is a lesson there.

Eerily smart and adaptable: The coyote

Coyotes are just pesky, wild dogs right? Not really. Often mistaken as a member of the Canid family (wolves, jackals, fox, and yes, domestic dogs – all plenty smart creatures), the coyote is of the Hyaenidae family and stands out for its ability to observe, take in information, problem solve, and adapt. They learn from experiences and can outsmart larger or more ferocious neighbors like wolves and badgers – even people.

Urban coyotes have been known to build dens and live right under people's houses without the residents even knowing. In town, they scavenge for food. Coyotes in a rain forest will live on berries and plants if other food sources are not available.

While the cheetah is designed for rapid acceleration to top speed, coyotes have a body built for marathons. They are not the fastest or strongest, but they are enduring. They are small compared to natural enemies so they are non-confrontational. They use their minds, not brute strength, to survive. And survive they do. Better than most animals, coyotes have learned to live in and around humans and flourish – even though many people would like to see them gone.

Coyotes are seen as pests precisely because they are so smart and flexible. Move a coyote to new surroundings, change the living conditions, introduce humans, and they will survive. Put them in the wild, be it a desert or a forest, they survive. Whether in East Los Angeles or Yosemite National Park, coyotes take in their surroundings, understand the opportunities and adapt. 'Survival of the fittest' is often thought of in terms of might. Coyotes demonstrate that 'fitness' can come from intelligence over strength and the ability to apply it to new requirements.

How many businesses have coyote-level flexibility to adapt and thrive?

As we learned in Chapter 2, customers and demand, even if well researched and measured, can be unpredictable and changing. Flexible performance chains have more ability to adapt as demand evolves, ebbs and flows.

Like the coyote, business flexibility can come in many forms. It can come from physical assets that are designed to easily adjust as demand flows in. It can come from smart processes that can observe or take in information as demand moves through the line and adjust as needed. It can come from a mix of fixed and variable elements, such as fixed work stations with variable staffing, or fixed skill sets with variable capacity. Together the mix creates the adaptable system. Flexibility enables problem solving before there is a problem!

Accommodating is not the same as flexibility

Often performance chains are rigid but 'management' or 'sales' or 'they' demand a solution for a customer. Nothing in the overall performance chain is adjusted to make that support requirement possible or permanent. Another demand comes in and that burden is added on top of the first. This happens again and again. Companies that get comfortable with this one directional push approach to meeting customer needs experience serious breakdowns between sales and operations. "Just make it happen" doesn't necessarily change the resources, process or tools. It doesn't consider the cost. It doesn't consider the strain on the system. Or people. The same standard things happen in the product or service development and then special handling kicks in. That is accommodation, not flexibility.

Accommodation is always expensive. It trains customers and

employees that exceptions are the norm. It chips away at the value proposition and eventually margins and profitability. Left to expand without some logic and creativity to introduce variability into the performance chain attributes, accommodation can be the complete undoing of a business. A coyote would never do that. Observing the first demand change, he would start adapting the system. If you see accommodation happening in your operations, start thinking about how to convert it to performance chain flexibility to get control of your destiny.

Too much and too little flexibility are both bad options

If there is too much performance flexibility, a company can lose focus trying to solve every need uniquely, even when it's unnecessary. As one example, I know a company that had thousands of envelope SKUs. Laying them side by side, you would be hard pressed to call out more than a half dozen differences. And that was just one of hundreds of product lines. Other companies create unique customer-product numbering combinations so even though the core products are essentially identical, they need to carry inventory and produce each one separately because the processes have been overbuilt to handle each and every variable. This isn't much of a problem when you're small and starting out. As you get larger, with more customers and more products, it becomes a tangled mess. Endless product variation running through your lines without some way to manage the complexity becomes a burden that is hard to unwind. The customer is often blamed for this complexity when, in reality, they aren't even aware of the gyrations the company has chosen to undertake 'on their behalf.' Had they understood, they might have asked for something different and saved both their own cost and company production cost.

Service organizations are not immune to this same flowering of complexity as more and more variables are added into service delivery. If controlling mechanisms aren't put into place, service level differences become hard to regulate and price. Pushed to the limit, a company has little choice but to take back from the customer something they themselves initiated. Usually the pendulum swings from complete flexibility to extreme limitations. As a consumer, you've seen this with banks, insurance companies, airlines, frequent user programs and more. From the option to pick any doctor or any clinic, to no coverage unless you're 'in network' with pre-approved appointments. From you can use your earned points anytime to black out days or other restrictions. Yes, you can use your debit card everywhere for free, until the day additional fees are imposed. Conveniently check your bags for a flight. Oh, but now there is a limit... and an additional cost for each bag. This is flexibility created and taken away when the system can't afford the handling costs.

What would the coyote do? Chances are he would have adapted the system as demand rose. Studying the volume and customer interest with his keen dispassionate eye, he would have moderated the performance chain before it got out of control. That is adaptation.

Not enough flexibility and you face loss of customers as others offer alternatives that you cannot provide. Traditional advertising-based companies experienced this as they tried to control customers while online businesses introduced all kinds of independence and customer buying power. Companies with too much cost tied up in fixed assets are hampered when new technologies and competitors change the game in an industry. They are caught flat-footed and restricted in ability to respond. The video companies that grew through bricks and mortar and now sit with expensive, underutilized locations are one good example.

Creating flexibility across the performance chain can best be captured in response time and cost to change. Interestingly enough, it can also come in the form of fixed systems and nimble systems.

As with speed and predictability, depending on your business model and value proposition, how you achieve flexibility can vary. And how much flexibility you need can vary. It isn't that more is always better. It isn't that complete flexibility is better.

Sometimes a fixed performance chain with the right inputs, outputs and processes provides the level of control you need so that you can be as flexible as you need to be to meet changing demand. We've seen this in manufacturing lines where the components are standardized but each car or motorcycle as an example comes off the line exactly as the customer ordered. In mail order pharmacy operations, the medications are standard, but each customer order is filled to exacting specifications. If you think of online shopping, the savvy retailers and media outlets know your interests based on past purchase and browsing patterns and tailor the information they send to you. The performance chain is fixed. The output is not.

In other cases, the performance chain needs high doses of empowerment, creativity and innovation to nimbly adapt, unrestricted by fixed investments. If you're in a professional services or consulting business as I am, each client – each engagement – has its own twists and turns. Flexibility to adapt based on input and circumstances is paramount. (See the interview with Richard Davis of U.S. Bank in the previous chapter, as another example.)

Both forms of flexibility, as well as variations in the middle, can be successful as long as they match your intention and as long as the entire performance chain understands how demand flows in, through, and out as efficiently as possible.

Establishing your need for flexibility

Flexibility, in the simplest performance chain terms, equals reductions in time and effort to convert processes to meet dynamic customer demands. How much time do you need to respond? Days, minutes? How much effort? Does it take the entire workforce or only specific functions or zones within your performance chain?

How can you best determine what kind and the degree of flexibility you need? Well, our friend Mr. Coyote has the answer. You need his exceptional observation skills. You need his ability to take in new information and calculate the impact on your business. You need his abandon and detachment from the current standard so that you can create a better new one. You need to be willing to move and use not only internal resources but also those available to you in your surrounding suppliers, vendors and other business partners. You need to adapt and establish a process that makes adaptation the norm.

To get your arms around current response times, your nimbleness and adaptability, as well as where you have immediate opportunities to increase flexibility, you can use the same operational excellence tools already discussed as well as new ones. And when it comes to flexibility, customer input is the most essential place to start. Flexibility, like speed, is too often viewed the same: more is better. And that can very often not be the case at all. More flexibility that customers value and will pay for is worth it. Here are a few ideas of ways to evaluate your flexibility performance and requirements:

- Quantitative and qualitative customer input – directly about your process and the translation to product or service benefits
- Value Stream and Zone Mapping can help you diagnose and focus on creating flexibility where you need it most. That might be in the number of stations, batch sizes, number of associates, or hours available. It might be in the number and types of exchanges between employees, and employees and customers. Mapping may lead you to a more comprehensive look at a sprawling supply or production chain – pushing for the answer to a basic question: Does it really have to be this complicated?
- Depending on the need you feel or the value of flexibility improvements to your operation, you might need to mine deeply by conducting detailed process studies. Done well, these kinds of process exams over a 2-day or longer period record exactly what

is happening. As the information is collected the key is to note what contributes to and what restricts flexibility.

- If you are a multi-product company and you need to accommodate many products running through the same operations, you may need a Change Over or Switchover Reduction assessment. The objective would be to identify improvements in process performance through analyzing and reducing the frequency and duration of switchovers from product to product, information system to information system, or batch to batch.
- If your flexibility comes more through your people than equipment or process changes, cross-training may be far more valuable than one more piece of equipment that adds capacity but no extra flexibility. Information and communications networks may be the solution rather than or only relying on tools and methods. Freedom from outdated standard operating practices may surprise you in how much flexibility you create. Empowerment to make decisions on defined accountabilities may do more for increased flexibility than any new process.

The world is getting more complex. Competition changes the rules daily. Customers are becoming savvier to their power in the marketplace. A flexible performance chain, balanced with speed, predictability and leverage is a must for future success. If you are wondering about your current state and how best to adapt to new demands and opportunities, here are a few questions to explore:

1. How do you track shifting market requirements (see the Steve Milligan interview in Chapter 3) so that you can anticipate and stay ahead of evolving flexibility requirements?

2. Do you know what kinds of and how much flexibility your customers will pay for? Are these requirements built into your new product or service development process?

3. What is the time to transition from one system, work type, or customer to another tracked? Are you satisfied with your conversion performance? If not, what can you do immediately to start collecting data?

4. What can you do to actively engage employees in reducing restrictions and time in all critical changeover processes?

5. Are current processes tied down by unique – and maybe unnecessary – customer plus product requirements? If so, are there activities to begin analyzing the value and cost of this complexity?

6. Do your staffing and skills development practices encourage creative problem solving or restrict employees to set work standards?

7. What kind of flexibility is most valuable to your operation? People flexibility? Process flexibility? Technology or tool and equipment flexibility? Do you have the capabilities in place to optimize your most important flexible resources?

Flexibility is hard to establish properly and even harder to evolve and adapt. That is why it is so important and so valuable. Rather than see our coyote comrade as a sneaky, willful pest, steal a few of his abilities, just as he would steal them from you!

Interview with Beth Sparboe Schnell, President, Sparboe Farms [18]

Bob Sparboe started the Sparboe Chick Company after returning from service in the Korean War. Originally a baby chick distributor, Bob sold day-old chicks to farmers in Central Minnesota. Today, with more than 55 years in the business, Sparboe Farms is the fifth largest egg producer in the country serving retail, wholesale and foodservice customers in 26 states. The core focus of Sparboe Farms is to service grocery distributors, retailers, foodservice restaurants, institutions and food processors who require superior quality eggs and egg products, both branded and private label. The company operates seven processing plants supported by 33 accompanying layer and pullet production sites it owns and operates in three states (Iowa, Colorado and Minnesota).

At the time of this interview, Sparboe Farms was actively defending itself following a news story, prompted by an animal rights group, that called into question the company's animal care practices. Beth Sparboe Schnell, daughter of the founder and company President, vowed to turn the crisis into an opportunity to do better. In part, she said:

> "Regrettably, these incidents should never have happened in the first place—but they did and we accept that responsibility. We were not as vigilant as we should have been in monitoring our farm employees to make sure that they were following our animal care code of conduct. However, we want to assure you that we are working around the clock to take corrective

measures by enhancing our animal care policies and procedures to make our company better... I helped my father build this business, and I'm committed to doing whatever it takes to support the good work of the vast majority of our employees who strive to do the 'right thing' every day."

Effectiveness of their performance chain, and how to make it better, was clearly on Beth's mind during our conversation.

Beth Sparboe Schnell grew up in her father's business. She worked for other companies after college and before returning to Sparboe Farms full time in 1985.

Let's start with your passion for the business:

"Certainly in my case I grew up in the business, watching my dad wrestle with it as it grew. Being a part of it my whole life, first as a part-time student and then coming back to the family business full time after some other corporate experiences.

"Even when I came back to the business in 1985 it was already a very different business from the one I grew up in. Back then our business was very local; our customers, local grocers, paid us cash out of the till. Today we have a wide variety of customers, many still local but also many national and international customers.

"I loved the simplicity of our business at one point and now I love the complexity. The challenges are greater and require much different leadership, management and execution skills. The work demands more of people at every level. It is dramatically different than when

I was starting out."

Talk about how you've grown the company

"Sparboe is a family business and this comes through in the way we work with our people – employees and our customers. The other day a customer said, 'You guys have always been an industry leader. Now others are catching up to you. What is your next deal?' I told him, 'Our innovations come from you and what you are working on. As one of your suppliers, what we do next is based on figuring out how we can help you do what you're trying to do, better.' Sometimes we see needs before customers see the needs. This is a strength of ours, to be attuned to our customers. We have to make sure whenever we invest, that we are adding value to the customer. It can't be just a great idea or one that only benefits us.

"We are also resilient. There is always an issue. It might be a disease outbreak, corn prices going up, or egg prices going down. We can't be rigid. We have to be resilient and tough."

Describe the challenges you've experienced in your time leading Sparboe

"Growth and scaling has been our challenge. It is not just adding more of the same. When my dad ran the company you could walk out in the yard and touch everything. But as you grow, the soft stuff needs to change, too. You're not just adding barns and equipment and systems. You are adding different kinds of skills.

"When you have multiple farms, you also have to evolve your

management structure. You have to establish procedures. You take an entrepreneurial company and have to put practices and procedures in place to do things right and to ensure you're delivering a consistent product to the customer. And you want to do it in a way that assures you do not lose all the good (entrepreneurial) stuff.

"Also in our business today, even versus just five or ten years ago, the regulatory requirements have increased and changed. It is way different than it was for my father. We have to make sure we are in compliance with evolving regulations.

"And, of course, customer demands and expectations change, which creates challenges."

When you think about your company's performance chain (or many performance chains) where do you start?

"Well, it starts with yield or production, making sure we are capturing and not wasting value all the way through the performance chain. Starting with: for every pound of chicken feed we buy, are we getting the right number of eggs? We have an intense focus on yield.

"Next I think about the complex collection of interrelated activities. In our business, it is not so many ingredients. It is having hands-on management making sure everything is done through the entire process.

"It all starts with good chickens and quality feed. The better we care for the chickens, the better we produce. The better we produce, the better our plants, processing and our distribution work.

"But, most of the challenges are with humans. We have to find people willing to work with animals and committed to carrying out our business values."

Can you relate to how speed, predictability, flexibility, and leverage play a role in the way Sparboe operates?

"For us, speed is most important in the customer order process. Given the perishable nature of our products, we need to be able to respond quickly. We pack our eggs every day out of the farms. The shorter the time from order to dock, the better. However, the shorter the lead time for the customer, the more challenging it is for us. It becomes a balance of customer satisfaction and plant efficiency. It also includes dealing with the challenges of a live bird in the process.

"Predictability shows up in sales as well. We know the heavy buying periods. For example, buying more eggs at Easter. The flocks are predictable. Other things throughout the process are not predictable. Something is always changing. In this business, you have to thrive in a chaotic world. It is a commodity world where the products are highly perishable and time is always a challenge.

"Flexibility is required for constantly changing requirements. We don't do things the way we did them three years ago. The source of the changes can be customers, competition, regulators, or consumer buying habits. This is a huge challenge – getting alignment across the growing enterprise and flexing to those changing requirements.

"Leverage in this business is about people. Our people are truly our greatest assets whether they work in nutrition, production or sales.

We are blessed with specialists that are really experts in key areas. Across the company, we tap into our specialists and leverage their knowledge."

Do you see these performance lenses in any priority order?

"Yes. Flexibility is definitely first, then leverage of people, next speed and finally predictability."

How do you drive the performance focus you want?

"By paying attention to #1. Who is accountable?

"Then communications is #2.

"Also through cross-functional teams. We've set up cross-functional teams to address challenges: customers, production, budgeting. This works really well. Sometimes it might take a 15 minute call but it makes a huge difference. The problem solving is done at the mid-management level. Sometimes the teams need to make recommendations. Other times a team gets together to assess the situation, decide and go."

How are these performance requirements balanced in the way Sparboe operates today?

"We are not characteristic of our industry. Most start with profitability. We start with production. We start with the output of eggs.

"When you're in a commodity business, people ask you all the time about profitability, but in our business it is not the best indicator of success. If you work in a widget company with high predictability, profitability might be a better indicator. However, we've had some years that were very profitable but I'm not satisfied with our performance. We've had other years where profit wasn't exactly where we'd like it to be, but I'm very satisfied because performance is doing what we need it to do. We focus on controlling what we can control to drive progress. Profit is an outcome of performance."

How do intangible characteristics of the performance chain show up at Sparboe?

"The best way I can explain it is through an example. We have some of our oldest facilities, with not the latest or greatest equipment, outperforming some of the more current facilities. The lesson here is that you can throw money at production all day long and not get the output you can from having the right people. It is the leadership and management that make the difference."

Talk about your customers

"Our goal, throughout our entire history, has been to focus on and understand our customers, regardless of size. We have regional and local customers that we value very much, and we have learned from and benefited from those relationships. We also have the large national and international customers, and learn from them as well. Some of our toughest buyers own smaller chains. Some of these guys operating regional businesses are really, really good. They push us and challenge us. Likewise, some of our largest, national/international customers bring us entirely different learning opportunities. We benefit from having a rich assortment of customers such as food service, retail, food stores, club stores, and national retailers."

Who are the other key stakeholders that most influence decisions you make within your performance chain?

"Feed suppliers, contract haulers that run our deliveries, the communities where we operate – where our farms and plants are located. This is important, not just because it is where our employees live, but also so we are seen as a good citizen. This is very important.

"Another thing we are working on is attracting new young people into the ag business. So we partner with schools that teach and train in agriculture, like the land grant universities and community colleges who are teaching tomorrow's leaders."

If I met a group of your most loyal long-term customers today, what would they say most differentiates Sparboe?

"I think they would say what I told you at the start. We gather a lot of customer feedback both in formal research and through direct conversations with them. Customers would view us as being a company that delivers what we say we are going to deliver. We are credible, capable, attentive, and extremely focused on their businesses. We are sincerely interested in their success.

"They would also say we are competitive. We wouldn't have the business we have without the right price, quality products, and efficiency."

Wrapping up – is there a final story or idea you want to share?

"Yes. Absolutely. We are back to people. Quite frankly it is the biggest challenge, the management intensity required for producing, processing and distributing a food product. You need to entrust employees to do the right thing – the business depends on it. This is especially important when it is your own family business.

"Then I think about the facts. The fact is that 98-99% of the time, our employees do the right thing, and customer orders are on time and accurate. Our hens produce safe, affordable, nutritious eggs for hundreds of customers in dozens of states, and we feed millions of Americans every day."

Leafcutter Ant, by San Diego Zoo

Chapter 6
Leverage

Rickie Ant stops by the cafeteria after the meeting and gathers up lunch for the whole colony. She knows they've been working hard while she's been away and probably hungry. She's going to need them to maintain their strength. All the work ahead of them is likely to increase. She knows her team is up to the task, but as she struggles

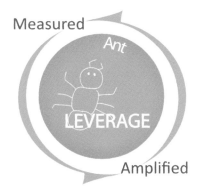

with the load she's delivering, she starts to imagine ways to get more done without burning everyone out or using up all the resources too quickly.

If you're this small, you need all the leverage you can get: The ant

It's true. Scientists generally agree that an ant can lift up to 20 times its body weight – with its jaws. That's like a human adult walking around carrying three full-sized cars with their teeth!

Ants are everywhere. They are one of the most abundant animals on the planet, and their contributions are important. They are fantastic engineers and born to work. They understood 'green' technologies long before humans – even creating natural air conditioning in their colonies with leaves and sticks. Living and working as they do with millions of their cousins, they have and rely on clear communications systems. Messages are sent by pheromones that are read by other ants using their antennae to interpret the important and specific messages. The news identifies the rank of the sender, can provide threat warnings to the colony, or be a call for cleanup duties in the passageways when some ants die and need to be removed.

Ants are social. There are over 14,000 varieties but all ants form colonies that range in size from a few dozen individuals living in small natural cavities to highly organized colonies which may occupy large territories and consist of millions of individuals. Ants live in a caste society and cannot break out of their assigned roles. They all have a job and work together for the greater good of the colony and, of course, the queen.

Their social structure is their strength and their weakness. The colony survives as long as the queen survives. Tear open their colony or mound and you literally have all their eggs in one basket.

Everyone contributes and everything is used in the ant world. That is leverage and that is a lesson for every business.

Leverage across the performance chain is about making more or doing more with existing resources and capital assets. Think of it as the productivity of fixed capital, working capital and labor. It can also mean additional financing or leveraging the balance sheet to fund growth, but for our performance chain conversation, let's stick to doing more with what we have. Let's make sure we get the most out of the capacity we have and the investment decisions we've already made – people, supply and distribution networks, raw materials, plants or branch facilities, and equipment – before we decide to spend or borrow more money. As someone I admired early in my career often said, "Assume there is no new money and see what you can do."

Too much capacity

When talking about excess capacity one thing needs to be clear: cost cutting and leveraging the performance chain are not the same thing. That may seem obvious, but it isn't always. When there is too much capacity, cost cutting is often the first act and seen as the more straight-forward option. This is essentially resetting assets and resources down against a lower level of anticipated opportunity. There is no doubt about it: cutting costs can be more painful but a relatively clean way to deal with excess capacity.

Cost cutting often, however, does more than trim the excess. It can make the performance chain weaker and impact demand generation if, as part of the decision process, the company trades true customer value for saving money. Remember the call center wait time story in the speed chapter. Short-term costs were saved but the demand spiral offset the cost reductions. There was no improvement in either the performance chain or customer benefits.

Using excess capacity takes a strategic behavior change and a committed effort to repurpose the resources and assets. Many companies sadly decide it is easier to just cut it out.

After decades of focus on productivity gains you would think all the excess would have been cut out or squeezed out of companies. And, true, many businesses have become masters at stretching resources. However, many others behave more like someone going on a fad diet – sharply cutting back and slimming down, only to balloon up again later. My theory, based on observations in the field over the past decade, is that this starving and binging behavior happens because the managers in these companies focus on cost cutting their way to better financial performance, not on leveraging their performance chain to better results.

Sometimes the market moves against a company and it is left with an aging product base and a performance chain that is too large, complex or overbuilt for the new demand requirements and market conditions. Cutting back in these situations is understandable. If a company can't find ways to use all their capacity, their only choice is to cut back.

An ant would never make the choice to cut. Ants only know more. More work. More output. More room for others. Leverage the colony, everyone and everything at their disposal. Growth is the only way.

If you find yourself in this situation with too much capacity the first two questions are:

1. Is this a short-term or long-term excess capacity problem?
2. Is there opportunity to use your resources and assets in new ways?

If your answer to the first question is that you have a short-term problem, leveraging your performance chain to cover the downturn with new or different activities preserves your strengths for the rebound. You're seeing many examples of this in flat economic times as companies hang on to key talent, and use a slow revenue cycle to perform maintenance and other fill-in work to see them through to a strong starting position as the market for their products or services returns. Cutting and then replacing initiates the binge cycle and weakens your starting place when things turn around.

If you determine that you have a long-term problem you may have to make cuts to reset your base. Assuming you do cut, the key will be to cut with a focus on future demand and opportunity. Your job is to preserve the resources and assets that give your performance chain strength and that can be leveraged into new opportunities. Too often cuts are made across the board or made without imagination and effort to strengthen the company with every decision. Addressing this second question takes some real work, but is worth it if, like an ant, your orientation is not just survival but growth of the business. You may, after pulling all the information together, decide that you really do not see any opportunities to use your excess capacity in new ways. If that is the case, you're back to cutting and the same rules apply as above.

The best option is to shift resources; move fixed and working capital and labor assets to other opportunities. One of the classic stories of U.S. entrepreneurialism is a perfect example of this kind of shift. During World War II, goods and services were rationed, capacity in manufacturing plants exceeded consumer demand, male workers were enlisting in the military and the U.S. government was desperately seeking war supplies. With government incentives serving as a hungry client, almost overnight many of those excess capacity resources were refashioned to provide munitions and other war support production. And, Rosie the Riveter went to work.

In other examples, whole companies have been reformed and grown by paying attention to customers using products in unintended ways. What was a satellite offering becomes the growth engine.

If you see opportunities to utilize your resources and assets in new ways, the heavy lifting of the performance chain change process begins. This is exactly the time when you need to tap the energy and creativity of your people and align their work and company resources to the new opportunities and requirements. It is also the time to look across the performance chain for the places where deep dive attention can serve as a lever to drive performance up and on to the new day.

Not enough capacity

Not enough capacity is much more enjoyable to think about. This is your opportunity to do more and perform better with the resources you already have in place. Not with the pain of cutting. And not with the pain of cracking the whip so everyone works harder. Leveraging your existing performance chain resources and assets is all about thinking differently and locating the pockets of opportunity across the performance chain that can release capacity and energy.

How do you go about finding pockets of opportunity in your performance chain? Typically companies, especially companies with growing demand, don't have obvious waste or excess resources sitting around unused. Processes are the way they are for a reason. Facilities and equipment are already aligned to the basic business requirements. People may already feel overtaxed so the thought of 'more' feels like punishment, not opportunity.

As with the other lenses, the key is to start with a diagnostic that provides the information you need to prioritize decisions. If you are going to do more with what you have and release capacity quickly, you can't change everything and likely don't need to touch every person, process and physical asset.

Assuming the demand opportunity and additional capacity needs are clear, start there. If not, the demand and supply plans need to be created and aligned. You need to know how much, what kind, when to deliver and any specific conditional requirements. This is when it is essential that your demand and supply leaders link pinkies and agree on the opportunity. No sales or marketing throwing a forecast over the fence to supply or operations. No operations resetting the plan based on what they will deliver rather than committing to the demand opportunity.

Whether your performance chain is vertically integrated and completely in your control, or includes outside suppliers or distributors, this is a time to get everyone on the same page. Aligning to leverage capacity without adding resources is a challenge when everything is under one roof. Magnify that challenge if you have a business with an expansive network of outsourced production, distribution or service centers. Add another multiplier if you're talking many geographies, time zones and languages. Whatever your current performance chain resources and assets, you have them for good reasons. Leveraging them is an opportunity to take advantage of the capabilities you have built.

Looking broadly and horizontally across your performance chain before you make your strategic capacity decisions will increase the likelihood that you'll spot great opportunities to hone in on and make dramatic leverage improvements without disrupting the entire chain. There may be one or two operations or sites which, if changed, can impact the flow of ins and outs across the entire chain. There may be key pieces of equipment that, used differently, can produce at higher rates. You may find employees who, if simply freed from burdensome processes, can improve their output. As in some of the other lens views, you will likely find historical or dated practices that can just be eliminated.

This is again time to start with what you know and add in detailed information that can pinpoint opportunities to create more leverage. The classic business book *The Goal*,[19] written and first published in 1984 by Eliyahu M. Goldratt, introduced the concept of 'Theory of Constraints." Still, 25 plus years later, when looking for ways to create more leverage, it is a great place to start. If you haven't read the book or studied Lean concepts, here are just a few examples that can get you on the road to finding more leverage in your operations:

Overall Equipment Effectiveness (OEE) or Overall Process Effectiveness (OPE)

If you need more capacity or output or both, and you're seeing bottlenecks in your performance chain, doing a Lean analysis called Overall Equipment Effectiveness (OEE) can help. Or if you are in a service business an Overall Process Effectiveness (OPE) analysis may be more helpful. Both can be powerful ways to reveal opportunities. OEE and OPE help you find those key pieces of equipment or process steps that if adjusted can immediately improve productivity. The machine may need adjustment. The process may need to change. And the manpower may need to shift. The reward is higher performance. There are many free OEE/OPE tools online and some applications you can buy for next to nothing. You can also do these calculations with a simple spreadsheet. What is important is to get accurate data from actual equipment or process measurements in real time – and to count everything.

Some OEE/OPE tools actually leave out or minimize the quality measurement. Doing so devalues the whole concept. Take your most critical machines or tools or process stages and complete an evaluation on them. From there you can identify specific improvement tactics that will measurably improve your quality rates, reduce downtime or lost time in critical phases of your work, and increase consistency of output. You do not need to apply OEE/OPE everywhere – only where you have the most critical need to even out predictability and/ or increase output.

48 Hour Studies are another way to conduct in-depth analyses of your operations, revealing detailed information of exactly what

is happening in a functional area or entire process over a two-day period. A longtime friend and client taught me years ago to clarify any situation or debate with the answer to this question: 'Do you think that or do you know that?' The whole point of a 48 hour study is to know the reality of what is really happening and reveal the opportunities that otherwise might go unnoticed. Done well, these kinds of exams collect the key information needed to make immediate leverage improvement decisions.

Find buried working capital

While you are taking a strategic or horizontal look across the performance chain at leverage opportunities, you may already know of some hot spots or bottleneck areas that need to be addressed. Using the same data-driven approaches discussed earlier, you can use focused projects to begin solving these challenges and start increasing system output through tactical changes. Consolidation of two good operations and teams into one super team and high performing operation can take single-digit improvements into high double-digit gains. Taking one day out of cycle time can be worth thousands to a small company and millions to a large one. Changing a process that holds up large receivables behind small ones is pure gold. These are all good business or operating practices. The company performs better. The added bonus is that these tactical adjustments typically release much-needed working capital. If some improvement investments in new equipment or people or capabilities are needed, it is far better to fund them through leverage of inside resources.

As with the other lenses, the quick assumption about leverage is that more is better. Sometimes that is true and sometimes it is not. I know one global professional services company that had pulled their human resources to the breaking point. The work was stretched so tightly across their performance chain that, like a rubber band fully extended, one more pull and the band would snap. They didn't need more leverage, they needed to measure the pressure they were putting on their system and insert some elasticity back into their work processes. Like too much speed, it is possible to over-leverage your resources.

Measured leverage may sound like an oxymoron, and for some businesses it is. For others, balancing the release of fixed and working capital and relying on people as the key leverage driver is fundamental to their operation. You've seen that in several of the interviews leading up to this chapter. Many companies continually find leverage in current operations and they do it on the left side of the continuum, in a measured way.

Other organizations need to amplify their leverage just to keep pace with the market. They sit on the right side of the continuum. You see this in young companies that have made it past the proof of concept stage and are now in a wild growth period. This is also true in many technology companies where there is significant pressure to drive down unit costs as volume explodes and production requirements go up and up and up.

If you need to address how effectively you are leveraging your current performance chain, here are a few questions to get you started:

1. Is your current concern too much capacity or not enough capacity to match your demand requirements?
2. Where are hot spots or constraint areas that you know about? What have you done to perform diagnostics on them (such as an OEE/OPE assessment or 48 hour study)? What hard data can you assemble to evaluate the cause and effect on either side of the constraints?
3. What is your leadership alignment like across the performance chain? What metrics, actions and forums allow for development of shared interests across functions?
4. Have you created a full inventory of the opportunities to consider as you develop strategies to do more with existing resources? If not, consider completing a zone map to get you started.
5. If you are considering resource cuts, have you protected the capabilities that will offer you the greatest leverage opportunities in the future?
6. What would one additional day of cycle time reduction be worth to you in freed up working capital?

Leveraging a business performance chain really is much like the ant colony that over time grows from thousands to millions, from a small mound to an entire ecosystem. Leverage comes from utilizing every resource; finding ways to release working capital to fund additional growth. In the colony, leverage comes from every ant doing its assigned job with the resources in front of it. In business it is constantly finding ways to make the work more productive across the entire company. Certainly at points there is a good case to be made for more investment, more new or outside capital. When those points occur, it's important to know that you're taking full advantage of the resources you already own.

Next time you see your highly leveraged friend the ant at a picnic, stop to admire his strength and selfless contributions to the greater good before you sweep him away.

Interview with Leigh Abrams, Chairman and Former CEO, Drew Industries, Inc. [20]

About Leigh Abrams

Leigh was the CEO of Drew Industries for almost 30 years. He is now the company Chairman of the Board of Directors and has been succeeded in the CEO role by Fred Zinn, the former CFO and his chosen successor. He credits many people, including Fred, but three other Drew leaders in particular, for the company's success to date. Rusty Rose, Drew's principal stockholder, former chairman and lead director, has been Leigh's mentor for more than 30 years. Rusty has been instrumental in keeping Drew focused on what needed to be done to be successful. David Webster, the CEO for almost 30 years of Kinro, Inc., a Drew subsidiary, until his retirement in 2008, and Jason Lippert, CEO of Lippert Components, Inc. another Drew subsidiary and since 2008, also CEO of Kinro Inc., have been critical to Drew's success. These two subsidiaries form the backbone of Drew Industries.

I met Leigh in midtown New York over a cup of tea on a very wet, cold day. I went into the interview armed with the background I'd received and the information available at the company website. I was expecting a pretty cut-and-dried manufacturing story. That is not at all what I got. As Leigh began to share the company story, the cold and wet day outside was lost in an incredible journey – and the warmth and openness of the man in front of me.

When we started, I made some initial comment about what a diversified company he led.

Leigh said, "Diversified?! No, we are really very focused – you should have seen us before!"

This is truly a story of leverage, as you'll see. Leveraging everything: from fixed assets to key investments; from personal and vendor relationships to talented and creative leaders; from a tight, well-honed manufacturing process to M & A deals; and adding in product innovation. And it all started with a bankruptcy. But before we go there, let's describe Drew Industries today, taken from the company website:

Drew Industries Incorporated (NYSE:DW), through its wholly-owned subsidiaries, Lippert Components and Kinro, supplies a broad array of components for recreational vehicles ("RVs") and manufactured homes. Drew's products include vinyl and aluminum windows, doors and screens, thermoformed products, steel chassis, chassis components, RV slide-out mechanisms and solutions, manual, electric and hydraulic stabilizer and lifting systems, entry and baggage doors, axles and suspension solutions, toy hauler ramp doors, furniture and mattresses, entry steps, and other towable RV accessories, as well as specialty trailers and related axles for hauling boats, personal watercraft, snowmobiles and equipment. From 31 factories across the United States, Drew is an important supplier to nearly all of the leading producers of RVs and manufactured homes. For the twelve months ended September 30, 2011 Drew had consolidated sales of $628 million, of which RV products accounted for 84% of consolidated net sales while manufactured housing products accounted for 16%.

Let's start at the beginning

Leigh came into the business as the assistant head of finance in the late '60s. He can't remember the title at the time (but knows they didn't have a CFO title then). At the time, the company was a real estate holding company. The owners decided to grow through diversification. When I asked Leigh what the Company then thought made a good acquisition candidate, he said: "Anyone who would sell to us." Not a great strategy by his own acknowledgement. As a result, the company went into bankruptcy.

At the time of the bankruptcy in 1975, the senior management team moved to Florida and left Leigh to take the company through the bankruptcy process. He did. It took 2 years. When Drew came out of bankruptcy, Leigh had only one really valuable asset, and it wasn't any of the physical assets in the portfolio.

He had a $15 million Capital Loss Carryover. With this single asset, he went looking for investors and the leverage story begins.

Through a friend and then partner at Peat Marwick, now KPMG, Leigh found his investors, but they put him through another test before they invested. They gave him a list of eleven tasks he needed to complete. He did them, all eleven, and nine months later, he got the investment, the old management team was asked to leave and Leigh was appointed President and CEO in 1979. He also got more than he bargained for. His company, Drew Industries, became a holding company for other acquisitions the investors wanted to make.

Throughout this period the Drew portfolio consisted of all kinds of companies – everything you might think of up to and including, at one point, a casino. Without focus, there was no leverage. With a stroke of brilliance (me saying this, not Leigh) he came up with the idea of separating an "old Drew" including everything that needed to be shed, from a "new Drew" that had at its core Kinro, Inc., a manufacturer of windows for RVs and manufactured homes, which Drew had acquired in 1980. From that point on, Drew began to focus and grow by focusing on the manufactured home and RV markets.

In 1997 Drew acquired Lippert Components, Inc., a manufacturer of components for RVs. Together these companies have created the product development capabilities and manufacturing disciplines to form the foundation of the company that exists today.

Drew continues to grow through acquisitions. Unlike many companies which acquire only to be unsatisfied with the results, Drew has a very tightly managed approach for evaluating candidates, concentrating on the valuable assets (typically the products) and integrating them into their existing performance chain. Everything else goes away.

What were the early challenges?

"In the early years, coming out of bankruptcy, the performance challenge was getting to cash flow. Then it became all about focusing the company – getting rid of a portfolio of companies that had no core alignment."

How have the needs evolved?

"Today Drew has high market shares so we are seeking strategic acquisitions that are adjacent to our core markets. The challenge now is finding growth opportunities that are natural extensions of our current business and integrating them into our operations."

If you think about Drew's performance chain (or many performance chains), what attributes come to mind?

"We innovate new products and components for our target markets. We lead the markets and are exceptional at translating customer needs into new product ideas. And we look for opportunities to acquire products or companies that can be integrated into our existing operations.

"We focus on cash flow and we keep corporate and operating overhead as low as possible."

Can you relate to how speed, predictability, flexibility, and leverage play a role in the way Drew operates? (Leigh is a storyteller and his details are meticulous. He doesn't speak in terms of a 'performance chain' but his stories are all about leverage, flexibility, predictability, and speed—in that order.)

- Leverage: "We have developed the capability to acquire companies, eliminate any unneeded management, sell off unneeded facilities, and reduce costs by putting the production of the new products into our operations that already are established and perform to our company standards. This leverages the operations and capital investments we have already made."
- Flexibility: "We have been creative in finding a way to make things work as new operations are acquired by Drew (or are sold) over

the years. And the chapters of Drew Industries are amazingly diverse. Even today, focusing on the RV and manufactured home markets still requires the flexibility to create and integrate a long list of products and components to serve those customers and build out adjacent market strategies."

- Predictability: "Having built a production model through Lippert and Kinro that is highly effective and profitable, this infrastructure creates the base for production of our core product lines and integration of new product opportunities."

- Speed: "Speed is most important in reacting to the market and being able to move production and sales to market segments that are growing quickly when a key segment, like manufactured homes, has peaked and has begun to decline."

Do you have a final story that sums up Drew and what makes your performance chain work?

"The quality and innovation that goes into each of our products is exceptional – and that is why we have the market share that we do. We pay attention to quality and service and to the details that matter in product differentiation. Most important we listen to what our customers want. Not just the physical properties, but what does it 'feel like' to use our products?

"Jason (the CEO of Lippert and Kinro) built Lippert through product genius and a deep understanding of the RV market and customers. He is a star at understanding markets, and not just the tangible functions or features of products, but also anticipating what the customer needs. We're not just making a door, for example – we think about 'access.' What will it feel like for the customer to walk through that door? Should we add lighting? Will it be easy to operate? Is it inviting, welcoming?"

Chapter 7
4 Lens Profile

Rashida Cheetah knows: speed at any cost becomes a negative.

Oralee Elephant can tell you: predictability delivered too late or for something that has lost market appeal is of little value.

Ace Coyote understands: flexibility that extends every process, decision or outcome is more harmful than helpful.

Rickie Ant reminds us: leverage of every resource to the nth degree will deteriorate performance and increase risk.

Depending on your company mission, strategy, customer experience requirements and value proposition, all four lenses:

- Are important. (Try naming a company that only needs one or two or three.)
- Matter differently to individual businesses. (Copying someone else is not recommended.)
- Need to exist in some balance to the others. (Across your entire performance chain.)
- Can detract if not aligned and managed well. (Just ask and observe your customers.)
- Underpin companies that *ROAR* with success. (Short term and long term.)

Understanding how speed, predictability, flexibility, and leverage show up in a business is what we call the "4 Lens Profile™." These organizational archetypes, if you will, form the basis of understanding a business' basic operating model. Not what company leaders say it is – but what it actually is in practice.

As you've read, the measurements for each lens include, but are more than, low to high or less to more. The rule for every business is not that more is always better. It takes an understanding of all four lenses individually and collectively to really understand what is driving current performance and what, if changed or adjusted, could improve performance.

On the right, you see continuums for each lens – again not bad to good, but described at each end by polarities or opposing principles, depending on what is important to the business.

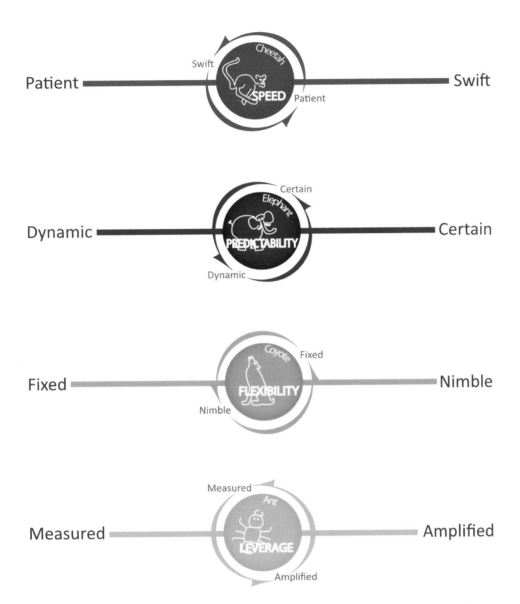

The icons in the middle represent a dial that you would move left or right depending on the need. In the interview with Steve Milligan, Chapter 3: Speed, he makes this exact point. Because markets are never static and customer needs are never static, you can't pick one position and stay there. Your business may always be on the left or right side of any of the continuums, but you are always adjusting based on the challenges and opportunities of the moment.

The last interview in the book, Chapter 8: Customer Experience with Jim Notarnicola, discusses the need to take the long view. Jim notes that if you are an established business, only adjusting based on what is directly in front of you is seldom enough. New competitors, technologies, innovations will rewrite the rules of an industry. Remaining viable may require completely rethinking your business model with significant adjustments to your speed, predictability, flexibility, and leverage positions.

If you're a new business just creating your performance chain, read the interview that follows in this chapter with Helen Ng, CEO of Planet Habitat. Like Helen, getting to the right balance of speed, predictability, flexibility, and leverage may take trial and complete restarts.

Where does your company fall along each continuum?

In Chapter 1 the phrase 'See the whole. Mine the meaningful.' was introduced. Using the 4 Lens Profile to assess the current state allows you to do exactly that. It creates an individualized profile for any company based on what is happening today. From it, you and other company leaders can decide if you like the profile and the results it drives – and/or which lenses if adjusted would most improve both business performance and deliver better customer experiences. These lenses taken together also provide new or cleaner language when describing or working on performance priorities across the business system that exists.

Everyone can understand the basic needs for speed, flexibility, predictability and leverage. Getting teams within or across work groups to agree on the priorities, mix and the balance required for success can move them out of any functional concerns or lenses into broader performance chain value creation.

All combinations can be good. Any particular lens or combination – like any set of polarities – can also be overdone. Mapping the 4 Lens Profile characteristics of a business on the continuums shown on page 143 creates one of the following profiles (knowing that each company is likely somewhere along each spectrum – not at the absolute end of any of them).

A simple (as in non-scientific) 4 Lens Profile can be developed easily through observation and scanning of readily available company information from press releases, interviews, analyst reports and marketing materials. There are seven interviews with leaders of seven very different businesses in this book. If you care to practice looking at a business through a 4 Lens Profile, read the interviews, check out their companies online, and see if you can plot where you would put them on the map on the next page. Use the continuum to create a profile for one of these organizations, or for your own!

What is your 4 Lens Profile?

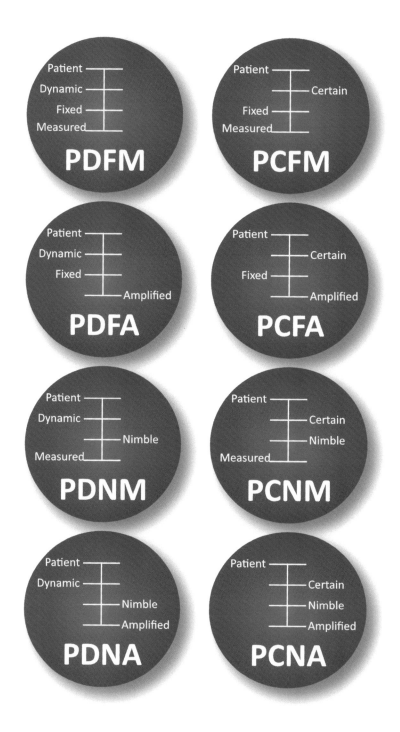

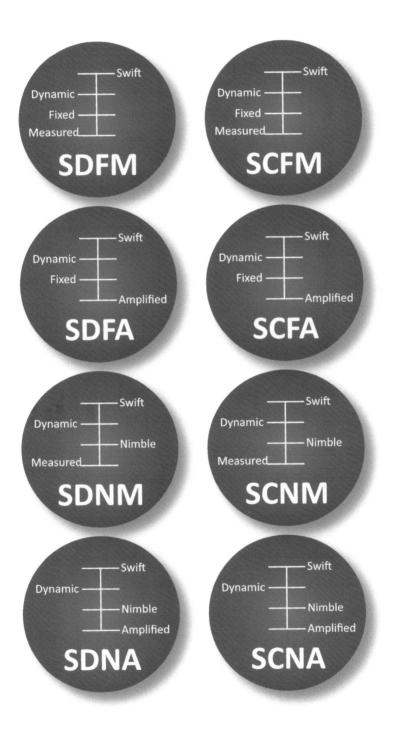

Below are a few examples:

This first example: Patient Speed, Dynamic Predictability, Nimble Flexibility, and Amplified Leverage (PDNA) might be a service organization where the performance chain has to be very responsive to specific customer input as value is created in the moment of service delivery.

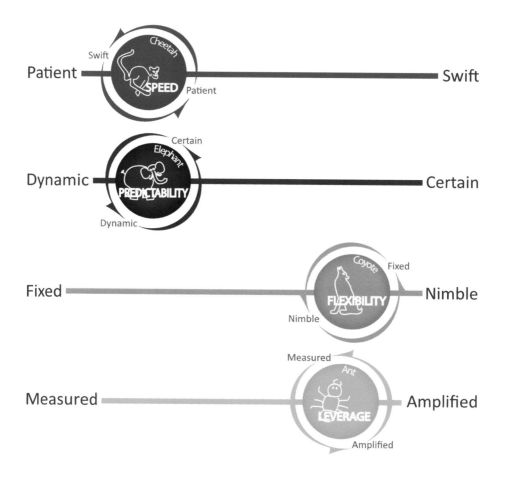

This next example: Swift Speed, Certain Predictability, Fixed Flexibility, and Amplified Leverage (SCFA) might be a global manufacturing company that has to orchestrate all the ins and outs of the performance chain across a complex and distributed supply chain.

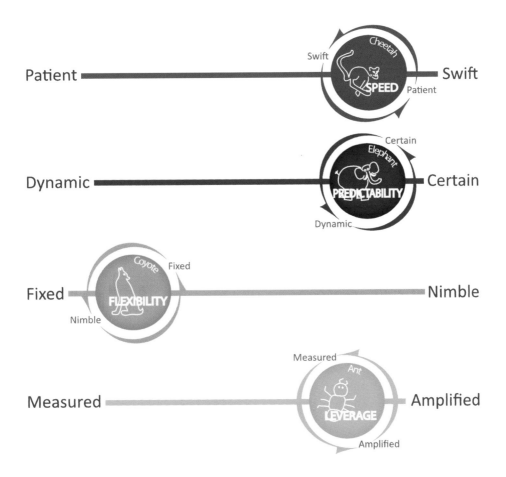

And a final example: Swift Speed, Dynamic Predictability, Nimble Flexibility and (slightly) more Measured Leverage (than Amplified) (SDNM) might be an online retailer where the performance chain infrastructure had to be built to support immediate response and adaptability based on customer behavior and purchase patterns.

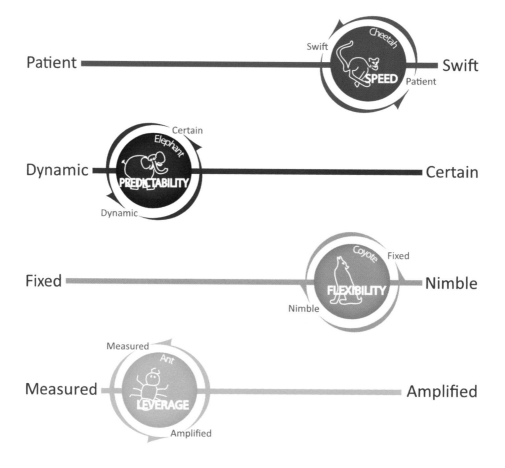

Creating a 4 Lens Profile that has real meaning that can be used to actually guide decision-making and investment decisions requires more information and analysis. This takes effort and calls for the use of a variety of tools, interviews and real time observations. Done well, a profile can guide you to the most important actions to boost your business performance. It can also reveal opportunities for innovation in your core processes. Establishing a routine of reviewing and adjusting the dials will help you identify essential trends that need attention. A good, fully informed profile of your performance chain includes both hard, quantitative data and qualitative assessments of your internal operations paired with your external customer experience.

What 4 Lens Profile is right for your business?

Rashida Cheetah Speed: Patient to Swift

Think about what defines your need for speed. Maybe you are in an industry that is driven by innovation or trends, such as technology or fashion. You have a need to stay with or ahead of the market, which drives you to the swift end of the continuum. Maybe your value proposition is to drive costs to the lowest possible point, requiring no excess time in value creation. That will push you to the swift end of the continuum. Like a cheetah, everything you do is designed to push the speed dial up.

If, on the other hand, what is really important to your business is deliberate and precise performance, say in the energy or communications world where there is zero tolerance for downtime, then a patient approach to speed is far more important. Throughput still may be very fast but is organized and managed in a metered way, like a cheetah preserving energy until the exact right moment.

Oralee Elephant Predictability: Dynamic to Certain

Dynamic predictability may seem like an oxymoron, but it is not. The important characteristic of a company at that end of the spectrum is the ability to predictably manage ups and downs in demand and absorb those changes in the performance chain without a loss of quality or output. Think of companies which, during certain seasons of the year, have long lead times and at other times of the year almost none. Consider how retailers operate ten months of the year versus the period over the peak holiday selling season. How even or uneven is the demand your company experiences? If there are market rumblings that require an immediate response, like our elephant friend, you need to dynamically transmit that information immediately into your operations.

If market success increases with certainty in your business, we will find you on the other end of the spectrum. If customers expect your company to be available 24 X 7, 365 days a year, then certainty is fundamental in at least critical segments of your performance chain. If product or service quality is an absolute requirement, for example in medical device businesses or pharmaceuticals or food businesses, the last thing you want is to issue a warning or recall. No margin for error or adjustment means you'll be way over on the certain end of the continuum, just like the elephants that walk the same path generation after generation.

Ace Coyote Flexibility: Fixed to Nimble

Fixed flexibility is another concept seemingly at odds with itself. But by design, some performance chains actually create the flexibility they need by grounding the basic foundations of their business in fixed principles, assets and processes. Organizations with significant fixed capital, whether manufacturing plants or service branches, drive flexibility using their assets to full advantage. The coyote doesn't change his core capabilities – they are fixed. He uses those capabilities to adapt as needed.

Nimble flexibility is more reflective of organizations that need lots of innovation and freedom to act at the point of sale or service. This kind of nimbleness is supported through technology and processes. In these environments employees are empowered to tailor a product or service request and equipped with the information and tools to act in the best interest of the company in the moment. This is just like the coyote who is not limited by or captive to his environment, his neighbors or any variations in his food supply.

Rickie Ant Leverage: Measured to Amplified

Most people know the grade school song about the ant and the rubber tree plant. If you recall the lyrics, "high hopes" is what an amplified performance chain is all about. Think of online businesses that in the past decade started in single product categories and today use the infrastructure they built for sales and distribution of an ever greater diversity of products and services. Peak performance comes from pushing the limits and driving the most out of all types of resources whether physical assets, people or processes.

At the other end of the spectrum are companies who utilize their resources in a more level way. Taxing resources for these businesses creates a wear factor and doesn't drive competitive advantage. If you're in a professional services business that is heavily dependent on people, for example, driving more hours per person doesn't necessarily contribute to performance improvement. There is a reason we want our airline pilots and surgeons well rested. Like the entire ant colony relying on everyone to carry out their assigned responsibility, these companies are stronger when the whole colony is more stable.

What side of each continuum is right for your business?

Once a company has this profile picture, leaders can assess whether they like what they see or if they need to make changes.

- Where are the matches and misses in the way the company actually works to drive performance and strengthen customer experiences versus the ideal target?
- How will you prioritize the adjustments you want to make? What criteria will you use?
- What about your performance chain is in alignment with your target customer experience and value proposition, and what works against it?
- Which attributes contribute positively to performance and which might be overdone and detract from the vision you have for the company?
- Where do real time activities match your company 'story' and where are they out of step?

Any company or organization that is more than a year or two old with more than two employees has developed a history. A culture has formed. Habits have or are becoming ingrained. You are now living with past decisions, good and bad. Prior capital investments and staffing decisions are in place and you need to get the most value and productivity from them.

All of these opportunities to see the company for what it is and mine meaningful change from targeted adjustments show up in the 4 Lens Profile.

Interview with Helen Ng, CEO, Planet Habitat[21]

Helen Ng and I met at a book discussion with a group of business CEO's in mid-town Manhattan. As she introduced herself and spoke about her company, I could see that what she is attempting to do with Planet Habitat® is massive and very exciting. At first, she and I both thought it might be premature to discuss Planet Habitat's performance chain because the organization is relatively young. On the other hand, thinking forward about performance requirements is a great thing to consider early. For anyone reading and contemplating a business startup or business reinvention, what Helen has to say may be particularly important.

When I called Helen for this interview, I had trouble keeping up with her rate of speech and thought. Hopefully I've done our conversation justice! I hung up the phone sure that this was a woman who will change the world.

A bit of background about Planet Habitat

From the first page of a simple, clear website you can see the magnitude of Helen's vision: "Investing in the 'Missing Middle.' Affordable Living for Tomorrow's Middle Class." The site lists initiatives in four focus areas: affordable housing, education, green infrastructure and community services.

Planet Habitat provides private equity and advisory services and describes itself as a "socially responsible U.S.-India initiative."

I wanted to talk to Helen for two reasons: 1) she needs her own effective performance chain to attract investments and execute the work of Planet Habitat, and 2) she is in a position to help a whole range of new companies in emerging markets build performance chains that will reshape and open opportunities for tomorrow's 'middle class' as she describes them.

About Helen Ng

"My mission in life is an expression of my experiences. It is simply about, 'What can I do with my set of skills to build bridges between the haves and have nots?'"

Helen is someone who has no problem thinking big and, as in the game of chess, strategizes several moves ahead of where she is today. She has a civil engineering and finance background and has done most of her work in emerging markets in infrastructure, housing and education. In her last job with a social venture fund, she was the global portfolio head of affordable housing. Over time she saw persistent gaps in the marketplace that the existing investment models were not equipped to address.

"From a practical standpoint, I thought the existing models were necessary but often limited as solution providers. There was room for a new model.

"As a result, I pulled my nerd hat on and thought about: 'How do you actually fix this?' I decided a new model needed to be created with an organizational, product and services overhaul and thus co-founded Planet Habitat with a partner in India."

What exactly is Planet Habitat?

"It is a global investment and advisory platform that supports the needs of the 'missing middle,' today's poor, tomorrow's middle class, in emerging markets. It is still evolving as a model itself."

Later in the interview, as you will see, Helen shared that this is the third iteration of Planet Habitat, which is an important point to note all by itself. Sometimes the right model or performance chain isn't obvious. Sometimes, particularly in startups and I would dare say in areas where there is no existing sustainable model such as the Planet Habitat universe, you need a willingness to try, adjust and if required, start over. It helps to have Helen's clear conviction about the long-term vision and her courage to try, let go, learn, and start again.

I placed this interview in this chapter on finding the right performance chain balance of speed, flexibility, predictability and leverage precisely because you have options. You can experiment your way to better performance no matter how new or longstanding your business. Every leader I spoke with talked about the need to adjust these lenses and adapt as business requirements and market conditions change.

Describe the services of Planet Habitat:

"There are three basic parts:

- A private equity fund – This is a baby right now. We use private capital and seek close-to-commercial returns.
- Advisory services or consulting – We offer domain specific advisory services. This has been around since 2000.

- Pluto – This is our not-for-profit arm. Pluto is the nickname. Through Pluto we use philanthropic money to provide grants for technical assistance. We also make program related investments through extremely patient capital."

You said the existing models are limited. What doesn't work?

"At one extreme of the capital spectrum, you have the traditional private equity and venture capitalists. Typically their terms are too demanding for the growing body of entrepreneurs serving the 'missing middle' in developing countries. Then if you look to the VC world, they are largely oriented towards technology. You don't usually don't see a VC involved in our niche sectors, particularly housing. So the organizational construct for this kind of work requires a different profile.

"At the other extreme, the philanthropic and NGO-driven social venture funds play a necessary role but often fall short for domains that are capital-intensive or require deep sector knowledge. For example, when most of the capital resources are philanthropic, there is a ceiling to how much you can raise and do using donated funds. In this economic age, if you take just one topic – housing – the ticket size is too big for such a model.

"Also, from an operational standpoint, there is too much dependence at such funds on the revolving door of young and mid-level managers, so you are constantly in a learning and retraining mode. Even if you correct that staffing model, you need to have your management team cognizant of the investment and domain requirements.

"We are balancing the types of investments, the levels, the culture match and the deal structure. This is a constant learning process. We are now on Version 3.0. I made mistakes, have retrenched and am continuing to refine the platform."

Can you say a bit more about those mistakes?

"My number one mistake was the people. This is a human services business. I picked people with the technical and financial skills but not a cultural or capability fit for this kind of an entrepreneurial environment. It took a couple hits to sense the better performers, but you really don't know until you're actually working together.

"Our philosophies were aligned, but when you get down to the basics: 'Can you actually produce the widget?' I found out, 'Actions speak louder than words.'

"Understanding this lesson has forced me to be very careful about who shares this plate with me at this stage.

"One of your lenses is leverage. This is key for us – staying small and proving our way in.

"Flexibility for us means that all the partners have to be as flexible as me. We need a mix of vision and shared accountabilities. The stew changes with the facts on the ground.

"As for speed, I do feel a time pressure. We want to respect the angel money from those that are supporting us, and that adds pressure to produce results quickly. At the same time we also need visible projects that are off the ground and that can establish the next level of investment and commitment.

"Predictability is not much of a factor in our operations today. We are a variation of what is unknown, so by definition not 'predictable.' We ourselves are inventing and putting our support behind others that are inventing. The balancing act is keeping the revenue as predictable as possible but only as much as we can without destroying the creativity and vision."

Can you give an example of a Planet Habitat project that will help create and support the 'missing middle?'

"Well, here is an example. This is an interesting candidate using bamboo for both housing construction and a bio-mass/green play. I like their approach. There are many bamboo companies, but they are small, local and not scalable. This one has a prefab scalable approach. They do quality projects that are aspirational. They are also interesting because they started as a non-profit. Now they are in their second year as a for-profit spin off. They are not just growing and selling bamboo. They are involving bamboo in its full ecosystem. *(A true performance chain!)* They see this opportunity as both a great product solution for better housing and as a way to help create jobs for people where they currently live.

"They now have around 500 artisans employed. These artisans can stay and work in their own rural communities rather than migrate to the cities. *(Flexibility!)* These artisans do a variety of work with the bamboo – treating, cutting, and shaping it into a variety of parts for the prefab line, or doing carvings, making the joints that will be installed a certain way, as examples.

"The company also has linkages to farmers. Adding bamboo plantings enhances the farmers' revenue streams and helps make each individual farm more predictable and reliable. *(Predictability!)*

"We like their management team. They have taken pains to create an assembly-line approach. They are outward looking – consciously looking for ways to grow the scale of the business. These guys have systems thinking and need to think this way to get to the level of building business across states in India. They do everything with an eye toward how it impacts their entire system. *(See the whole. Mine the meaningful!)* Their competitors are more entrenched in a small, nepotistic model that can only grow so much.

"This is a good example of the kinds of projects Planet Habitat is interested in. It has a blended approach. They have an organizational construct to their 'assembly line.' Walking into their warehouse is a great example: the bamboo is inventoried, sized, very organized and neat; you go to another section of the warehouse where they might be putting together a roof truss and all the pieces are together with experts doing the assembly.

"In India there is huge economic pressure to go to the urban areas to find work. Many want to stay in the rural areas but are forced to leave. Helping companies like this to grow opens a choice to stay home."

Let's go back to your own performance chain. Where are you at in your own development process?

"We've gone through some dry runs. I would say from the first round the lessons are about streamlining the investment process. Early on we were presented with an opportunity to invest in, but not all of our own players marched in sync. As a result, we dragged too long, strayed from a deductive process, and became culturally inconsistent with our end customers. In this market, you have to be more disciplined and culturally aligned.

"Second lesson is to absolutely pay more attention to the management teams of our candidate portfolio companies and not just what they are currently doing but also their own human dynamics. We have to see a certain level of ability and flexibility. Whatever is in the plan will meet bumps. We need to see their resiliency and ability to work through changing requirements."

Have you set long-term goals?

"We have a global vision, but our markers are short term. We don't know how long it will take to move from our little petri dish to something that is fully developed. My thinking is in 3 – 6 – 9 month increments. We need to have realistic, tangible outcomes that we have delivered on, and grow from there.

"As an example, when we started we were covering India and West Africa. From a practical standpoint, that was just too much. Now we are keeping our work in India until we are established and proven.

"Our advisory services are different. For those we are open to a wider market and that exposure keeps us sharp."

What would you like readers to understand about Planet Habitat?

"I would like them to know this:

- We are building a very well thought-out professionalized approach using financial innovation to address the needs of tomorrow's middle class in emerging markets.
- We are actually trying to balance the intersections of 3 types of ecosystems through our performance chain: a demographic ecosystem, sector-specific ecosystems, and a fund ecosystem.
- We are working on ourselves. We are designing the organizational framework and construct to solve: How do the economic incentives within this organization work as one whole so we select the right people, our workers are aligned, we don't have the traditional revolving door, and we minimize the politics? We have to imbed the culture and performance requirements of the company into the DNA from the get-go.
- Finally, this is a true Rubik's cube!"

A Pause in the Experience, Japan, by Linda Ireland

Chapter 8
Customer Experience

This is a book about improving performance by focusing on speed, predictability, flexibility, and leverage as value is created, moves in, through and out of an entire performance chain. As you've read throughout the book, it is a common mistake to make business choices about improvements independent of any consideration for the impact on customer experiences. The business leaders interviewed for *ROAR* couldn't be more different or run a more diverse set of companies, and yet each of them spoke (without prompting) to the need for a tight integration of customer requirements into every decision – and then updating these requirements in your performance chain as the market changes and experiences dictate.

There is a reason the performance chain model (below) introduced in Chapter 1 shows the customer experience like an arrow through every phase of operations. Customer experience needs to be inextricably imbedded in what you do at every stage of performance. It drives your need for speed, predictability, flexibility, and leverage. It is the key ingredient to determining the 4 Lens Profile that will serve your organization best.

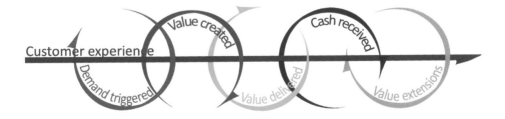

You have a customer experience whether you plan it or not. Why not plan and then execute the best one possible? Roaring performance only happens when, as the definition says:

> All the tangible and intangible elements move together from the moment you trigger demand until you have cash in the bank; all the ins and outs work together and align to your target customer experience to drive the outcomes you want.

Theodore Levitt, an economist and Harvard business professor, said when he wrote the famous article "The Marketing Imagination" in 1983: "The purpose of a business is to create and keep a customer."[22] In some records the original quote was supposedly: "The only true purpose of a business is to get and keep a customer."

I like the original better but in either case, the focus seems right. Peter Drucker also gets credit for saying something similar (although later than Levitt's article): "The purpose of a business is to create a customer." Both men were giants in the field of understanding business and more than capable of delivering lesson upon lesson about business, leadership and management. The fact that they agreed on this basic precept has been something I've carried with me throughout my career.

I had the opportunity to meet Mr. Drucker in the mid-1990s. Along with a small group of work colleagues, we had the opportunity to sit with him for a private visit at The Drucker Institute at Claremont Graduate University. It was a meeting I will always cherish. Long into his 80s at the time, still sharp and full of ideas and questions, one of the topics in our small group discussion with him was customer experience.

I'm reminded of that conversation as this discussion of performance chains comes together with customer experiences. I agree with Levitt and Drucker that the purpose of a business is to create and keep a customer. A high-functioning performance chain that goes into motion as demand is created and completes when value is delivered and customer needs evolve is perfectly in line with this philosophy.

The performance chain definition is grounded in demand, and demand only exists if there is a customer. Demand is triggered when a person who has a need enters the market to find an answer. For it they will trade their time, trust, and money. Demand, as you read in Chapter 2, is integral to, but different than, customer experience. Demand and customer experience bookend this discussion of performance chains because they frame the purpose of all the decisions you make along the way to create and capture value.

Customer experience is what happens to an individual and how they feel as they:

- Realize a need,
- **Learn** about their options to solve the need,
- **Try** out options,
- **Buy**,
- **Solve** their problem or need, and
- **Evolve** to another need over time.

Customer experience matters because it directly impacts the level and quality of demand. This is true whether an individual is solving a need for themselves, their family or a friend, or putting their reputation on the line as they make a decision that will impact their business.

So while the customer is learning, trying, buying, solving, and evolving – your business/your performance chain must:

- **Earn** consideration
- **Demonstrate** that you are the best option to solve their need
- **Protect** the customer as they buy
- **Prove** your promise through the product or service you provide, and
- **Anticipate** their next need.

In a picture, the two sides of the experience look like this:

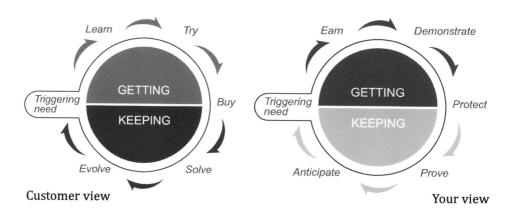

Customer view   Your view

Customers constantly enter and exit the market. Someone gets them and, if they are lucky, keeps them. This cycle repeats over and over again, whether you're thinking consumers or business customers. How effectively your performance chain works dictates whether you're getting and keeping (and growing) customers – or getting, losing, and replacing customers which we all know is an expensive proposition.

Customers reward and penalize companies based on their experience. If the experience is great, demand is enhanced and the likelihood of loyalty and repeat business increases as needs repeat and evolve. This creates more opportunities for growth. If the experience is bad or terrible or just less than expected, demand dries up. And the reasons for good and bad experiences are endless. Just to name a few obvious candidates:

- The product or service works or doesn't work as promised
- Delivery was on time or late
- The customer felt understood and valued or like a number, just the next in line
- The customer finds you easily in the marketplace or misses you completely – maybe you are prospecting at the wrong watering hole!

If the performance chain works and the experience delivers real value, both you and the customer win. If the performance chain misses by a little or a lot, both you and the customer lose. Even if the customer has continuing needs, they will take their demand elsewhere and the opportunity for growth diminishes.

Decisions and actions across the performance chain have everything to do with whether the experience is positive or negative. If your speed decisions are Rashida Cheetah spot on; if your predictability is of Oralee Elephant quality; if you can adapt as Ace Coyote would to evolving needs; and if your costs and service reflect the full leverage of your resources as Rickie Ant would do, the likelihood that you will get and keep and grow customers goes up. The likelihood is that your profitability will increase, too.

A company 4 Lens Profile may or may not be visible and likely does not matter to the customer. But it does impact their experience. Speed, predictability, flexibility, and leverage and how you choose to implement them across your performance chain directly impact your customer experiences. The impacts can be negative or positive, rarely if ever neutral. At the highest level, what matters to a customer is: did they get their need or problem solved in a way that worked effectively for them? How well your performance chain works is the key to a positive answer.

What the customer sees, feels, tastes, touches, and smells is the sum of every decision that was made along the performance chain. There is a lot more that can be and needs to be said about customer experience. What is important as a wrap to this book is that customer experience drives demand and is the external manifestation of your performance chain effectiveness.

If you know whether your customer experience is making you money or costing you money, you can use those insights to focus on performance chain enhancements. If you don't know the true state of the experience you provide, finding out is important. It is as important as any other performance chain diagnostic you might perform.

If you don't know or aren't sure whether your performance chain decisions are contributing or detracting from the target experience you want to provide, here are a few final questions to explore:

1. What defines your target experience?
   a. Is it product quality?
   b. Ability to tailor at the point of transaction?

    c.   Allowing the customer to do for themselves?

    d.   Lowest possible cost with no frills service?

    e.   Maximum convenience (defined by the customer?)

    f.   Other...

2. Are your customer satisfaction scores going up or down?

    a.   Can you isolate the issues that are contributing to change in your scores?

    b.   Do they point you to speed, predictability, flexibility, or leverage challenges?

3. Anecdotally, what do you hear from your employees who are not in direct contact with customers? Do they have any sense of their impact on the ultimate experience you deliver?

4. What, if changed inside your company, would have the single most positive impact on your customers? What's holding you back from making this change?

One last interview follows that pulls the performance chain into a customer experience relief. After that, we'll see if **Rashida Cheetah**, **Oralee Elephant**, **Ace Coyote,** and **Rickie Ant** have learned to work together.

Interview with Jim Notarnicola, Red Mango Executive, Investor and Entrepreneur[23,24]

To introduce Jim is difficult because he is not one thing – he is many things. He is not with one company, he has involvements with several. Brock Capital where Jim is a Senior Managing Director describes Jim this way:

(Jim is an) "Expert in retail and restaurant marketing and franchise operations. Former EVP and Chief Marketing Officer, Blockbuster, Inc., 7-Eleven, Inc.; Currently President, Nicely Bros. Ice Cream Distribution; and a Partner in J&B Restaurants, Inc. (Red Mango)."

At Red Mango, Jim is currently Director of Domestic and International Licensing. Jim says in his typically understated way, "I've bounced around a lot. Consider me a retail marketing guy and an investor in both retail and distribution businesses."

So unlike the other interviews, this one is about Jim's experience in several businesses with differing performance chain challenges. He is a fitting interview for closing the customer experience chapter because it is his passion. A customer experience discussion was my first introduction to Jim many years ago, and it will invariably come up in every conversation. It is core to the way Jim thinks about business and performance requirements, much like the first interview in the book with John Dunlap at the San Diego Zoo. Jim was an advisory board member to my company, Aveus, and though not officially on the board now, he is still one of the first calls I make if I need a candid, clarifying point of view. (In addition, as you will soon see, Jim did this interview having already read the book, which was his request!)

Describe your passion for retail businesses

"Retail is immediate response. You go to market on a small scale and you either find a market or don't. If you do, you scale from there. It is interesting now with online businesses, you can literally follow from your demand trigger.

"You respond and iterate immediately based on what your customers are valuing and asking for. You can scale your business with direct interaction. I enjoy working in this kind of performance chain.

"I've dealt with retail at every stage of retail evolution. Way back with 7-Eleven, I started when we had 5000 stores and left when we had 30,000 worldwide. And during this same time we were being overrun by the other alligators. Back then, gasoline sellers were converting to C-stores. We were in a robust business where there was huge consumer demand. But as we learned, there were a lot of other players in the watering hole, to use your market analogy.

"The market turned on the prime real estate of gasoline stations and the convenience need. The trigger for gas stations converting to C-stores was the gas rationing at the time. Rationing cut down on the economics of these businesses so they were forced to do something else to survive. They started adding groceries. We (at 7-Eleven) were arrogant. We focused on the small stations and didn't believe they could ever figure out groceries. What we completely missed was their prime real estate and the consumer need for more and more convenience. As long as consumers were stopping for gas, the stations might as well sell them other stuff as well. At 7-Eleven, we didn't have the real estate to bring in gasoline. If we could have seen the long-term trend, the store strategy would have been completely changed.

"From this experience, one of the things I always think about is something (Peter) Drucker wrote about: how companies miss changes over the long run. Even companies who are cheetah-like fast, or coyote-like flexible, tend to react to things right in front of them but fail to step back and see the changes in the long view."

What about a situation where you do understand the shifting marketing dynamics?

"Blockbuster was interesting in that regard. When I joined them it was already apparent that the market was evolving. We understood the challenge. The concept of streaming media was just an idea, but we knew it was coming. This, however, was pre-DVD and no one had enough broadband at the time to stream. While there was the vision of streaming, people were just wrapping their minds around switching from tape to DVD. DVD alone re-excited the category because the quality was so much better. Our job at the time was going in and re-merchandizing, converting the stores from tape to disc and applying lots of retail marketing methods to the locations. Just by doing that we doubled the revenues in the first 3 years. We also realized that competing meant being a player in the media-to-home/media-streaming business. We saw that this change would leave us with this big inventory of retail stores that would need repurposing. Like the elephant metaphor, we were really efficient and predictable at moving packaged media to locations. When we tried to make the conversion to media-to-home, we could not really get there.

"I'm not sure where this fits, but you see it time and again: companies hold on and hold on to their operating model or performance chain until others do them in or force a change. My question is, 'How do mature companies summon the will to adapt to the point where they out-compete their core business?'"

You're right, we see this all the time. Do you have a thought or answer for that challenge?

"Companies need to try to keep their focus way out to the outer-edge of customer experience. We need to underscore being customer-driven, to get around the customer experience of the business we are already in and pay attention to what customers are telling us is coming and needed. To be truly observant to what they are telling us.

"Leaving the big corporate world and getting involved in Red Mango, I'm in the other seat. We are reinventing a major category: at the macro level, frozen food and at the more category specific or micro level, frozen yogurt. So here is a case: why couldn't the existing lead player see that people want REAL yogurt, healthy yogurt? It took newcomers to see this trend. The new players, like Red Mango, are in the process of scaling while the existing category is being left behind."

Retail performance requirements have changed a lot with the growth in online. How do you see this affecting performance chain decisions?

"Online businesses and all subscription businesses, talking from my retail perspective, carry a heavy burden. In traditional retail, switching is very, very easy. If a customer doesn't like the merchandise or service in one store, they simply walk down the block or to another store in the mall. Now with online businesses and services, God forbid I change my bank, my movie set up or setting preferences for any of my regular sites with any business where I'm building a history. All the things these companies did to make the online businesses wonderful are the same things that makes the customer extremely angry when the company does something heavy handed and without regard to customer concern. In the online watering hole, everyone is competitor, customer, and potential partner. And customer retribution is swift. In the online world there is total authority at the point of the end customer. You have to be listening to what is said and unsaid. Ignore the signs at your own peril. It is the global and virtual version of the watering hole and everyone knows instantly what is in and out."

Can you relate to how speed, predictability, flexibility, and leverage play a role in your company performance chain as Red Mango grows?

Speed: "When my investment group got into the Red Mango business, what we said was 'This is all about being fast to market – all about speed.' There are low barriers to entry. And our customer behavior is established; they are very familiar with the category. What is being offered is far superior to older offerings for the same price: a healthy alternative in line with the food trends of today. We knew it, that speed would be critical, but even knowing it we haven't been able to go as fast as possible. As a result, new entrants have moved in, for example another chain and some mom & pops. While we've grown very rapidly, we haven't been able to maintain the market share we wanted. So now we are working on ways to grow faster and still maintain our quality.

Predictability: "Like any business with a high quality perishable product, we have our operations people pushing to keep quality and ensure operations controls as we grow.

Flexibility: "In any retail situation, you are responding to a category that is being defined by competitors and where customers give you immediate feedback. You have to be able to absorb that information as it comes in and adapt.

Leverage: "For Red Mango, I think about leveraging the existing customers who are already buying in the category. We can leverage that knowledgeable, experienced customer, just by raising the quality of the product. The other big leverage point in retail is buying power as we grow. For us that critical leverage point is between 250 and 500 stores. At that scale, it all comes together: buying power, market presence, etc. Before that inflection point in any retail operation, you are completely stretched for resources. One of the new things we have been able to leverage is the proliferation of social media. Historically, in a business like this we would spend 10 X what we spend on marketing now. Today, because of the profile of our customer (young, educated, connected) almost all of our marketing is social, where customers drive the demand by sharing with others.

"Every business has a different type of opportunity under each of the four lenses."

In business assessments we talk about the tangible and intangible characteristics that drive performance. What are the intangibles in the Red Mango experience?

"What runs through my mind about intangibles is the idea that we've invested in creating a store environment that allows customers to 'take a break for themselves.' No matter what they buy, whether a frozen yogurt, a parfait or a smoothie, about 70% are 'dining in.' They are there to refresh themselves. So we are focusing our brand development to allow people to feel refreshed.

"As one example, we have to train staff so they understand how to do things that fit the customer's need or opportunity to refresh. The big intangible is the nature of trust, to operate in ways that the customers can trust the experience to be true to the promise."

Any final thoughts about where customer experience is going and how it will impact business performance chains?

"An interesting theme that runs through all the business experiences I've had is letting customers 'do it for themselves.' If I go all the way back to 7-Eleven and the introduction of ATMs, we had the intersection of knowledge, technology, and availability. As consumers, we've all concluded that we'd rather do it for ourselves. Even in the frozen yogurt business, we started by serving the customer. We were doing the presentation. Now we're turning the machines around and letting the customers serve themselves because that's what customers want. They want to do it for themselves. They want their own special twist and through their direct involvement, they help us co-create new ideas or improvements. Across our network, the stores we've changed to self-serve are outperforming the original stores. This plays havoc with the model, but it really does come down at the end to: you better be good at being 'coyote' adaptable. Maybe you have a reason for wanting to do something for the customer, to serve them, but there is more potential in setting up the performance chain so they can serve themselves.

"Imagine a whole globe of customers empowered to do for themselves: build my own retail company, make my own tools, develop my own processes, and have the ability to access unlimited resources and information. How do you set up your business performance chains to enable that? I see that this open-sourced creativity is where the next great innovations will come from to drive businesses and economies."

Afterword

The CEO called another meeting, this time at the watering hole. She wants to celebrate the dramatic turnaround in company performance. The company is running ahead of the competition. Revenue and profits are up and market share is growing. Analysts are positive and the stock is a recommended 'buy.' Customer satisfaction has evolved to more meaningful loyalty and experience metrics and they are all headed north. Good work is everywhere you look, not just in isolated cells. Employees are happy and energized – the whole company feels different. This is no joke. Some version of this performance description is happening somewhere. It could be at your company.

Rashida Cheetah sprints to his spot by the water and says, "Geez boss, thank you! It is a lot more fun to be on this side of the performance curve, and I have to tip my hat to you, Oralee, Ace and Rickie. What a team! (And I don't even LIKE teamwork!)"

Oralee Elephant, predictably appearing with her herd close behind, says, "In all my memory I don't recall better performance." A deep rumbling in the herd confirms her statement. "I'm so glad we were able to invite everyone along to celebrate."

Ace Coyote, off to the side, watching and listening, finally steps up for a drink and chimes in, "You're wonderful. Sorry I called you idiots before. The change and increase in flexibility since we've all had our lenses adjusted and started solving problems together has been amazing. Who knew I could not only get along with, but actually end up enjoying working with you! Our customers have never been happier with us. Cheers!"

Last but not least, leveraged high above the heads of a line as far as the eye can see, **Rickie Ant** arrives on a throne of leaves and sticks like Cleopatra. Smiling and laughing, she says, "What a great way to work! It's so nice to be appreciated! Rare for us to stop but we just had to come and celebrate."

Peace (and prosperity!) at the waterhole tonight.

Footnotes and Links

1. http://www.aveus.com/what_we_do/education/taming_the_performance_chain/

2. http://supurna.com/

3. http://www.aveus.com/what_we_do/our_expertise/performance_chain_excellence/

4. http://industryweek.com/articles/tame_your_performance_chain_22821.aspx

5. http://www.laurieexcell.com/blog

6. http://www.aveus.com/what_we_do/our_expertise/customer_experience/

7. http://www.aveus.com

8. Wegeforth, H.M. & Morgan, N. 1953. It Began with a Roar: the Beginning of the World-Famous San Diego Zoo (revised edition). (California: Crest Offset Printing Company)

9. http://www.sandiegozoo.org/90th/index.html

10. http://www.sandiegozoo.org/

11. http://www.gregdutoit.com

12. http://www.gregdutoit.com/index.php?page=ftf blood

13. http://www.diannepix.com/

14. http://en.wikipedia.org/wiki/Value_stream_mapping

15. http://www.hitachigst.com/company/

16. http://www.usbank.com/index.html

17. Flight of the Buffalo: Soaring to excellence, learning to let employees lead. (by James Belasco and Ralph Stayer)

18. http://www.sparboe.com/

19. The Goal: A Process of Ongoing Improvement by Eliyahu M. Goldratt, Jeff Cox

20. http://drewindustries.com/

21. http://planethabitat.net/

22. http://rites-of-passage.com/images/Levitt_TheMarketingImagination.pdf

23. http://www.redmangousa.com/default.html

24. http://www.brockcapital.com/

CPSIA information can be obtained
at www.ICGtesting.com
Printed in the USA
271820LV00001B